# THE CULTURE MAP

# THE
# CULTURE MAP

*BREAKING THROUGH THE INVISIBLE
BOUNDARIES OF GLOBAL BUSINESS*

ERIN MEYER

**PublicAffairs**
*New York*

Published in the United States by PublicAffairs™,
a Member of the Perseus Books Group

PublicAffairs books are available at special discounts for bulk purchases
in the U.S. by corporations, institutions, and other organizations. For
more information, please contact the Special Markets Department at
the Perseus Books Group, 2300 Chestnut Street, Suite 200, Philadelphia,
PA 19103, call (800) 810-4145, ext. 5000, or e-mail special.markets@
perseusbooks.com.

*Book Design by Cynthia Young*

Library of Congress Cataloging-in-Publication Data
Meyer, Erin.
    The culture map : breaking through the invisible boundaries of
  global business / Erin Meyer.
      pages cm
    Includes bibliographical references and index.
    ISBN 978-1-61039-250-1 (hardback)—ISBN 978-1-61039-259-4
  (e-book)   1. Diversity in the workplace.   2. Psychology, Industrial.
  3. Interpersonal relations.   I. Title.
HF5549.5.M5M494 2014
658'.049--dc23

                                                2013048509


First Edition

10 9 8 7 6 5 4 3 2 1

*This book is dedicated to my sons, Ethan and Logan,*
*who show me daily what it means to grow up across cultures,*
*and to my husband, Eric, who made this all possible.*

# CONTENTS

# Navigating Cultural Differences and the Wisdom of Mrs. Chen

When dawn broke that chilly November morning in Paris, I was driving to my office for a meeting with an important new client. I hadn't slept well, but that was nothing unusual, since before an important training session I often have a restless night. But what made this night different were the dreams that disturbed my sleep.

I found myself shopping for groceries in a big American-style supermarket. As I worked my way through my list—fruit, Kleenex, more fruit, a loaf of bread, a container of milk, still more fruit—I was startled to discover that the items were somehow disappearing from my cart more quickly than I could find them and stack them in the basket. I raced down the aisle of the store, grabbing goods and tossing them into my cart, only to see them vanish without a trace. Horrified and frustrated, I realized that my shopping would never be complete.

After having this dream repeatedly throughout the night, I gave up trying to sleep. I got up, gulped a cup of coffee and got dressed in the predawn dark, and wound my way through the empty Paris streets to my office near the Champs Elysées to prepare for that day's program. Reflecting that my nightmare of ineffectual shopping might reflect my anxiety about being completely ready for my clients, I poured my energy into arranging the conference room and reviewing my notes for the day ahead. I would be spending the day with one of the top executives at Peugeot Citroën, preparing him and his wife for the cultural adjustments they'd need to make in their upcoming move to Wuhan, China. If the program was successful, my firm would be hired to provide the same service for another fifty couples later in the year, so there was a lot at stake.

Bo Chen, the Chinese country expert who would be assisting with the training session, also arrived early. Chen, a thirty-six-year-old Paris-based journalist from Wuhan, worked for a Chinese newspaper. He had volunteered to act as a Chinese culture expert for the training, and his input would be one of the most critical elements in making the day a success. If he was as good as I hoped, the program would be a hit and we would get to conduct the fifty follow-up sessions. My confidence in Chen had been bolstered by our preparatory meetings. Articulate, extroverted, and very knowledgeable, Chen seemed perfect for the job. I had asked him to prepare two to three concrete business examples to illustrate each cultural dimension I would be covering during the program, and he had enthusiastically confirmed he would be ready.

Monsieur and Madame Bernard arrived, and I installed them on one side of the big glass rectangular table with Chen on the other side. Taking a deep, hopeful breath, I began the session, outlining on a flip chart the cultural issues that the Bernards needed to grasp so their time in China would be a success. As the morning wore on, I explained each dimension of the key issues, answered the Bernards' questions, and carefully kept an eye on Chen so I could help facilitate his input.

But Chen didn't seem to have any input. After finishing the first dimension, I paused briefly and looked to him for his input, but he didn't speak up. He didn't open his mouth, move his body forward, or raise his hand. Apparently he had no example to provide. Not wanting to embarrass Chen or to create an awkward situation by calling on him when he was not ready, I simply continued with my next point.

To my growing dismay, Chen remained silent and nearly motionless as I went through the rest of my presentation. He nodded politely while I was speaking, but that was all; he used no other body language to indicate any reactions, positive or negative. I gave every example I could think of and engaged in dialogue with the client as best I could. Dimension after dimension, I spoke, shared, and consulted with the Bernards—and dimension after dimension, there was no input from Chen.

I continued for three full hours. My initial disappointment with Chen was spilling over into full-fledged panic. I needed his input for the program to succeed. Finally, although I didn't want to create an awkward moment in front of the client, I decided to take a chance. "Bo," I asked, "did you have any examples you would like to share?"

Chen sat up straight in his chair, smiled confidently at the clients, and opened up his notebook, which was filled with pages and pages of typed notes. "Thank you, Erin," he replied. "I do." And then, to my utter relief, Chen began to explain one clear, pertinent, fascinating example after another.

In reflecting on the story of my awkward engagement with "Silent Bo," it's natural to assume that something about Chen's personality, my personality, or the interaction between us might have led to the strained situation. Perhaps Chen was mute because he is not a very good communicator, or because he is shy or introverted and doesn't feel comfortable expressing himself until pushed. Or perhaps I am an incompetent facilitator, telling Chen to prepare for the meeting and then failing to call on him until the session was almost over. Or maybe, more charitably, I was just so tired from dreaming about lost fruit all night long that I missed the visual cues Chen was sending to indicate that he had something to say.

In fact, my previous meetings with Chen had made it clear to me that he was neither inarticulate nor shy; he was actually a gifted communicator and also bursting with extroversion and self-confidence. What's more, I'd been conducting client meetings for years and had never before experienced a disconnect quite like this one, which suggested that my skills as a facilitator were not the source of the problem.

The truth is that the story of Silent Bo is a story of culture, not personality. But the cultural explanation is not as simple as you might think. Chen's behavior in our meeting lines up with a familiar cultural stereotype. Westerners often assume that Asians, in general, are quiet, reserved, or shy. If you manage a global team that includes both Asians and Westerners, it is very likely that you will have heard the common Western complaint that the Asian participants don't speak very much and are less forthright about offering their individual opinions in team meetings. Yet the cultural stereotype does not reflect the actual reason behind Chen's behavior.

Since the Bernards, Chen, and I were participating in a cross-cultural training program (which I was supposed to be leading—though I now found myself, uncomfortably, in the role of a student), I decided to simply ask Chen for an explanation of his actions. "Bo," I exclaimed, "you had all of these great examples! Why didn't you jump in and share them with us earlier?"

"Were you expecting me to jump in?" he asked, a look of genuine surprise on his face. He went on to describe the situation as he saw it. "In this room," he said, turning to M. and Mme. Bernard, "Erin is the chairman of the meeting." He continued:

> As she is the senior person in the room, I wait for her to call on me. And, while I am waiting, I should show I am a good listener by keeping both my voice and my body quiet. In China, we often feel Westerners speak up so much in meetings that they do this to show off, or they are poor listeners. Also, I have noticed that Chinese people leave a few more seconds of silence before jumping in than in the West. You Westerners practically speak on top of each other in a meeting. I kept waiting for Erin to be quiet long enough for me to jump in, but my turn never came. We Chinese often feel Americans are not good listeners because they are always jumping in on top of one another to make their points. I would have liked to make one of my points if an appropriate length of pause had arisen. But Erin was always talking, so I just kept waiting patiently. My mother left it deeply engrained in me: You have two eyes, two ears, but only one mouth. You should use them accordingly.

As Chen spoke, the cultural underpinnings of our misunderstanding became vividly clear to the Bernards—and to me. It was obvious that they go far beyond any facile stereotypes about "the shy Chinese." And this new understanding led to the most important question of all: Once I am aware of the cultural context that shapes a situation, what steps can I take to be more effective in dealing with it?

In the Silent Bo scenario, my deeper awareness of the meaning of Bo's behavior leads to some easy, yet powerful, solutions. In the future, I can be more prepared to recognize and flexibly address the differing cultural expectations around status and communication. The next time I lead a training program with a Chinese cultural specialist, I must make sure to invite him to speak. And if he doesn't respond immediately, I need to allow a few more seconds of silence before speaking myself. Chen, too, can adapt some simple strategies to improve his effectiveness. He might simply choose to override his natural tendency to wait for an invitation to speak by forcing himself to jump in whenever he has an idea to contribute. If this feels too aggressive, he might raise his hand to request the floor when he can't find the space he needs to talk.

In this book, I provide a systematic, step-by-step approach to understanding the most common business communication challenges that arise from cultural differences, and offer steps for dealing with them more effectively. The process begins with recognizing the cultural factors that shape human behavior and methodically analyzing the reasons for that behavior. This, in turn, will allow you to apply clear strategies to improve your effectiveness at solving the most thorny problems caused by cross-cultural misunderstandings—or to avoid them altogether.

\* \* \*

When I walked into Sabine Dulac's second-floor office at La Defense, the business district just outside of Paris, she was pacing excitedly in front of her window, which overlooked a small footbridge and a concrete sculpture depicting a giant human thumb. A highly energetic finance director for a leading global energy company, Dulac had been offered a two-year assignment in Chicago, after years of petitioning her superiors for such an opportunity. Now she'd spent the previous evening poring over a sheaf of articles I'd sent her describing the differences between French and American business cultures.

"I think this move to Chicago is going to be perfect for me," Dulac declared. "I love working with Americans. *Ils sont tellement pratiques et efficaces!* I love that focus on practicality and efficiency. *Et transparent!* Americans are so much more explicit and transparent than we are in France!"

I spent several hours with Dulac helping her prepare for the move, including exploring how she might best adapt her leadership style to be effective in the context of American culture. This would be her first experience living outside France, and she would be the only non-American on her team, twin circumstances that only increased her enthusiasm for the move. Thrilled with this new opportunity, Dulac departed for the Windy City. The two of us didn't speak for four months. Then I called both her new American boss and later Dulac herself for our prescheduled follow-up conversations.

Jake Webber responded with a heavy sigh when I asked how Dulac was performing. "She is doing—sort of medium. Her team really likes her, and she's incredibly energetic. I have to admit that her energy has ignited her department. That's been positive. She has definitely integrated much more quickly than I expected. Really, that has been excellent."

I could sense that Webber's evaluation was about to take a turn for the worse. "However, there are several critical things that I need Sabine to change about the way she is working," Webber continued, "and I just don't see her making an effort to do so. Her spreadsheets are sloppy, she makes calculation errors, and she comes to meetings unprepared. I have spoken to her a handful of times about these things, but she is not getting the message. She just continues with her same work patterns. I spoke to her last Thursday about this again, but there's still no visible effort on her part."

"We had her performance review this morning," Webber said with another sigh, "and I detailed these issues again. We'll wait and see. But if she doesn't get in gear with these things, I don't think this job is going to work out."

Feeling concerned, I called Dulac.

"Things are going great!" Dulac proclaimed. "My team is terrific. I've really been able to connect with them. And I have a great relationship with my boss. *Je m'épanouis!*" she added, a French phrase that translates loosely as "I'm blossoming" or "I'm thriving." She went on, "For the first time in my career I've found a job that is just perfect for me. That takes advantage of all of my talents and skills. Oh, and I have to tell you—I had my first performance review this morning. I'm just delighted! It was the best performance review I have had since starting with this company. I often think I will try to extend my stay beyond these two years, things are going so well."

As we did with the story of Silent Bo, let's consider for a moment whether the miscommunication between Webber and Dulac is more likely a result of personality misfit or cultural differences. In this case, national stereotypes may be more confusing than helpful. After all, the common assumption about the French is that they are masters of implicit and indirect communication, speaking and listening with subtlety and sensitivity, while Americans are thought of as prone to explicit and direct communication—the blunter the better. Yet in the story of "Deaf Dulac," an American supervisor complains that his French subordinate lacks the sophistication to grasp his meaning, while the French manager seems happily oblivious to the message her boss is trying to convey. Faced with this seemingly counterintuitive situation, you might assume that Webber and Dulac simply have incompatible personalities, regardless of their cultural backgrounds.

So you might assume. But suppose you happened to be speaking with twenty or thirty French managers living in the United States, and you heard similar stories from a dozen of them. As they explained, one by one, how their American bosses gave them negative feedback in a way they found confusing, ambiguous, or downright misleading, you might come to the correct conclusion that there is *something* cultural driving this pattern of misunderstanding. And in fact, such a pattern does exist—which strongly suggests that the case of Deaf Dulac is much more than a matter of personality conflict.

This pattern is puzzling because Americans often *do* tend to be more explicit and direct than the French (or, more precisely, more "low-context," a term we'll explore further in a later chapter). The one big exception arises when managers are providing feedback to their subordinates. In a French setting, positive feedback is often given implicitly, while negative feedback is given more directly. In the United States, it's just the opposite. American managers usually give positive feedback directly while trying to couch negative messages in positive, encouraging language. Thus, when Webber reviewed Dulac's work using the popular American method of three positives for every negative, Dulac left the meeting with his praise ringing delightfully in her ears, while the negative feedback sounded very minor indeed.

If Dulac had been aware of this cultural tendency when discussing her job performance with her new American boss, she might have weighed the negative part of the review more heavily than she would if receiving it from a French boss, thereby reading the feedback more accurately and potentially saving her job.

Armed with the same understanding, Webber could have re-framed his communication for Dulac. He might have said, "When I give a performance review, I always start by going through three or four things I feel the person is doing well. Then I move on to the really important part of the meeting, which is, of course, what you can do to improve. I hate to jump into the important part of the meeting without starting with the positives. Is that method okay for you?"

Simply explaining what you are doing can often help a lot, both by defusing an immediate misunderstanding and by laying the foundation for better teamwork in the future—a principle we also saw at work when Bo Chen described his reasons for remaining si-lent during most of our meeting. This is one of the dozens of con-crete, practical strategies we'll provide for handling cross-cultural missteps and improving your effectiveness in working with global teams.

## INVISIBLE BOUNDARIES THAT DIVIDE OUR WORLD

Situations like the two we've just considered are far more common than you might suspect. The sad truth is that the vast majority of managers who conduct business internationally have little under-standing about how culture is impacting their work. This is espe-cially true as more and more of us communicate daily with people in other countries over virtual media like e-mail or telephone. When you live, work, or travel extensively in a foreign country, you pick up a lot of contextual cues that help you understand the culture of the people living there, and that helps you to better decode communication and adapt accordingly. By contrast, when you exchange e-mails with an international counterpart in a country you haven't spent time in, it is much easier to miss the cultural subtleties impacting the communication.

A simple example is a characteristic behavior unique to India—a half-shake, half-nod of the head. Travel to India on business and you'll soon learn that the half-shake, half-nod is not a sign of disagreement, uncertainty, or lack of support as it would be in most other cultures. Instead it suggests interest, enthusiasm, or sometimes respectful listening. After a day or two, you notice that everyone is doing it, you make a mental note of its apparent meaning, and you are able henceforth to accurately read the gesture when negotiating a deal with your Indian outsourcing team.

But over e-mail or telephone, you may interact daily with your Indian counterparts from your office in Hellerup, Denmark, or Bogota, Colombia, without ever seeing the environment they live and work in. So when you are on videoconference with one of your top Indian managers, you may interpret his half-shake, half-nod as meaning that he is not in full agreement with your idea. You redouble your efforts to convince him, but the more you talk the more he (seemingly) indicates with his head that he is not on board. You get off the call puzzled, frustrated, and perhaps angry. Culture has impacted your communication, yet in the absence of the visual and contextual cues that physical presence provides, you didn't even recognize that something cultural was going on.

So whether we are aware of it or not, subtle differences in communication patterns and the complex variations in what is considered good business or common sense from one country to another have a tremendous impact on how we understand one another, and ultimately on how we get the job done. Many of these cultural differences—varying attitudes concerning when best to speak or stay quiet, the role of the leader in the room, and what kind of negative feedback is the most constructive—may seem small. But if you are unaware of the differences and unarmed with strategies for managing them effectively, they can derail your team meetings, demotivate your employees, frustrate your foreign suppliers, and in dozens of other ways make it much more difficult to achieve your goals.

Today, whether we work in Düsseldorf or Dubai, Brasília or Beijing, New York or New Delhi, we are all part of a global network (real or virtual, physical or electronic) where success requires navigating through wildly different cultural realities. Unless we know how to decode other cultures and avoid easy-to-fall-into cultural traps, we are easy prey to misunderstanding, needless conflict, and ultimate failure.

## BEING OPEN TO INDIVIDUAL DIFFERENCES IS NOT ENOUGH

It is quite possible, even common, to work across cultures for decades and travel frequently for business while remaining unaware and uninformed about how culture impacts you. Millions of people work in global settings while viewing everything from their own cultural perspectives and assuming that all differences, controversy, and misunderstanding are rooted in personality. This is not due to laziness. Many well-intentioned people don't educate themselves about cultural differences because they believe that if they focus on individual differences, that will be enough.

After I published an online article on the differences among Asian cultures and their impact on cross-Asia teamwork, one reader commented, "Speaking of cultural differences leads us to stereotype and therefore put individuals in boxes with 'general traits.' Instead of talking about culture, it is important to judge people as individuals, not just products of their environment."

At first, this argument sounds valid, even enlightened. Of course individuals, no matter their cultural origins, have varied personality traits. So why not just approach all people with an interest in getting to know them personally, and proceed from there? Unfortunately, this point of view has kept thousands of people from learning what they need to know to meet their objectives. If you go into every interaction assuming that culture doesn't matter, your default mechanism will be to view others through your own cultural lens and to judge or misjudge them accordingly. Ignore culture, and you can't help but conclude, "Chen doesn't speak up—obviously he doesn't have anything to say! His lack of preparation is ruining this training program!" Or perhaps, "Jake told me everything was great in our performance review, when really he was unhappy with my work—he is a sneaky, dishonest, incompetent boss!"

Yes, every individual is different. And yes, when you work with people from other cultures, you shouldn't make assumptions about individual traits based on where a person comes from. But this doesn't mean learning about cultural contexts is unnecessary. If your business success relies on your ability to work successfully with people from around the world, you need to have an appreciation for cultural differences as well as respect for individual differences. Both are essential.

As if this complexity weren't enough, cultural and individual differences are often wrapped up with differences among organizations, industries, professions, and other groups. But even in the most complex situations, understanding how cultural differences affect the mix may help you discover a new approach. Cultural patterns of behavior and belief frequently impact our perceptions (what we see), cognitions (what we think), and actions (what we do). The goal of this book is to help you improve your ability to decode these three facets of culture and to enhance your effectiveness in dealing with them.

## EIGHT SCALES THAT MAP THE WORLD'S CULTURES

I was not born into a multicultural family to parents who took me around the world. On the contrary, I was born outside of Two Harbors, Minnesota, most famous among drivers on the road leaving Duluth as the home of Betty's Pies. It's the kind of small town where most people spend their entire lives in the culture of their childhood. My parents were a bit more venturesome; when I was four, they moved the family all of two hundred miles to Minneapolis, where I grew up.

But as an adult I fell deeply in love with the thrill of being surrounded by people who see the world in dramatically different ways from me. Having now lived nearly half of my life outside of the United States, I've developed skills ranging from learning to eat mopane worms for an afternoon snack while teaching English to high school students in Botswana, to dodging cows, chickens, and three-wheeled rickshaws during my morning run while on a short-term executive teaching stint in India.

Today, married to a Frenchman and raising two children in France, I have to struggle with cross-cultural challenges daily. Is it really necessary for an educated person to fold lettuce leaves before eating them, or would cutting the lettuce also be acceptable? If my very kind upstairs neighbors kissed me on the cheeks when I passed them in the hall yesterday, would it be overkill for me to kiss them on the cheek the first time I pass them every single day?

However, the lessons in this book emerged not from discussions about lettuce leaves or mopane worms (interesting as these may be), but from the fascinating opportunity to teach cross-cultural management in one of the most culturally diverse institutions on earth. After opening the French branch of a cross-cultural consulting firm, where I had the pleasure of learning from dozens of culture specialists like Bo Chen on a daily basis, I began working as a professor at INSEAD, an international business school largely unknown in Two Harbors, Minnesota.

INSEAD is one of the rare places where everyone is a cultural minority. Although the home campus is located in France, only around 7 percent of the students are French. The last time I checked, the largest cultural group was Indian, at about 11 percent of the overall student body. Other executive students have lived and worked all over the world, and many have spent their careers moving from one region to another. When it comes to cross-cultural management, these global executives are some of the most sophisticated and knowledgeable on the planet. And although they come to INSEAD to learn from us, every day I am secretly learning from them. I've been able to turn my classroom into a laboratory where the executive participants test, challenge, validate, and correct the findings from more than a decade of research. Many have shared their own wisdom and their tested solutions for getting things done in a global world.

This rich trove of information and experience informs the eight-scale model that is at the heart of this book. Each of the eight scales represents one key area that managers must be aware of, showing how cultures vary along a spectrum from one extreme to its opposite. The eight scales are:

- *Communicating*: low-context vs. high-context
- *Evaluating*: direct negative feedback vs. indirect negative feedback
- *Persuading*: principles-first vs. applications-first
- *Leading*: egalitarian vs. hierarchical
- *Deciding*: consensual vs. top-down
- *Trusting*: task-based vs. relationship-based
- *Disagreeing*: confrontational vs. avoids confrontation
- *Scheduling*: linear-time vs. flexible-time

Whether you need to motivate employees, delight clients, or simply organize a conference call among members of a cross-cultural team, these eight scales will help you improve your effectiveness. By analyzing the positioning of one culture relative to another, the scales will enable you to decode how culture influences your own international collaboration and avoid painful situations like the one in which Webber and Dulac found themselves caught.

## PUTTING THE CULTURE MAP TO WORK

Let me give you an example of how understanding the scales might play out in a real situation. Imagine that you are an Israeli executive working for a company that has just purchased a manufacturing plant in Russia. Your new position requires you to manage a group of Russian employees. At first, things go well, but then you start to notice that you are having more difficulty than you did with your own Israeli staff. You are not getting the same results from your team, and your management style does not seem to have the positive impact it did at home.

Puzzled and concerned, you decide to take a look at the position of Russian business culture on the eight scales and compare it

**FIGURE I.1.**

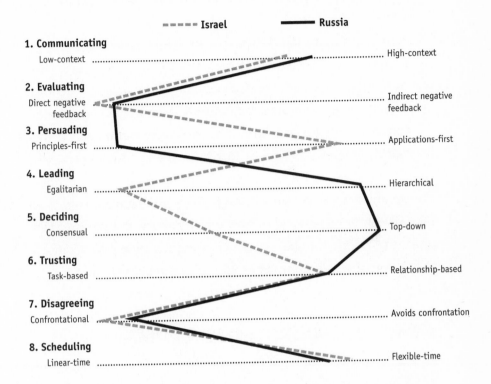

with Israeli culture. The result is the culture map shown in Figure I.1—the kind of tool we'll explore in detail in the chapters to come.

As you review the culture map, you notice that Russian and Israeli business cultures both value flexible scheduling rather than organized scheduling (scale 8), both accept and appreciate open disagreement (scale 7), and both approach issues of trust through a relationship orientation rather than a task orientation (scale 6). This resonates with your experience. However, you notice that there's a big gap between the two cultures when it comes to leading (scale 4), with Russia favoring a hierarchial approach, while Israel prefers an egalitarian one. As we'll discuss in more detail later, this suggests that the appreciation for flat organizational structures and egalitarian management style so characteristic of Israeli businesspeople may be ineffective in Russia's strongly hierarchical environment.

Here is a clue to the difficulties you've been having. You begin to reconsider the common Israeli attitude that the boss is "just one of the guys." You realize that some of your words and actions, tailored to the egalitarian Israeli culture, may have been misunderstood by your Russian team and may even have been demotivating to them. In the weeks that follow, as you begin to make adjustments to your leadership style, you find that the atmosphere slowly improves—and so do the bottom-line results. This is an example of how we use the eight scales and the culture mapping process to effect genuine, powerful changes within organizations, to the benefit of everyone involved.

## HOW DID MY COUNTRY GET PLACED THERE?

Each of the following chapters is devoted to one of the eight culture map scales. Each scale positions twenty to thirty countries along a continuum and guides you in applying the scale to dozens of situations commonly arising in our global business world. Because what is important on the scale is the relative gap between two countries, someone from any country on the map can apply the book's concepts to their interactions with colleagues from any other country.

Some may object that these scales don't give adequate weight to cultural variations among individuals, subcultures, regions, and organizations. Understanding how the scales were created may help you see how such variations are reflected in the scales, as well as how you can most accurately apply the insights that the scales provide.

As an example, let's look at the placement of Germany on the Scheduling scale, which reflects how people in various cultures tend to manage time. The first step is interviewing mid-level German managers, asking them to speak about the importance of being flexible versus organized when it comes to scheduling meetings, projects, or timelines. Of course, individual responses vary, but a normative pattern emerges. A bell curve illustrates the range of what is considered appropriate and acceptable business behavior on the scheduling scale in Germany, with a hump where the majority of responses fall. It might look like this:

**FIGURE I.2.**

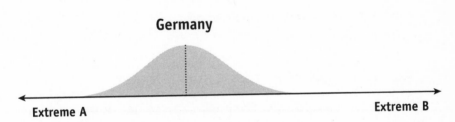

Of course, there are probably a few outliers—a handful of Germans who fall to the right or the left of the hump—but their behavior, judging by the average German's opinion, would be considered inappropriate, unacceptable, or at least not ideal in German business culture.

It was through this type of analysis that I began to map the country positions on each scale. I later adjusted the positions based on feedback from hundreds of international executives.

When you look at the scales depicted in this book, you won't see the hump for each country, but simply a point representing the normative position of the hump, as shown in Figure I.3. In other words, the country position on the scale indicates the

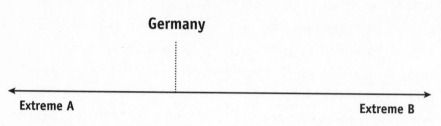

FIGURE I.3.

Germany

Extreme A                                    Extreme B

mid-position of a range of acceptable or appropriate behaviors in that country.

When you look at the scales, keep in mind that both cultural differences and individual differences impact each international interaction. Within the range of acceptable business behaviors in a given culture, an individual businessperson will make choices in particular situations.

For example, consider the Evaluating scale (see Chapter 2), which deals with whether it is better to be direct or indirect when giving negative feedback. There is a range of acceptable ways to give negative feedback in the Netherlands, and a Dutch business-person can comfortably make a choice that falls anywhere within that range. Similarly, there is a range of appropriate ways to give negative feedback in the United Kingdom, and a British business-person can choose a specific approach from any place within that range (see Figure I.4). The culture sets a range, and within that range each individual makes a choice. It is not a question of cul-ture *or* personality, but of culture *and* personality.

If you compare two cultures, you may find that portions of their ranges overlap, while other portions do not. So some Dutch people might employ feedback styles that are appropriate in the Netherlands as well as in the United Kingdom, while others may use techniques that seem acceptable in the Netherlands but would

**FIGURE I.4.**

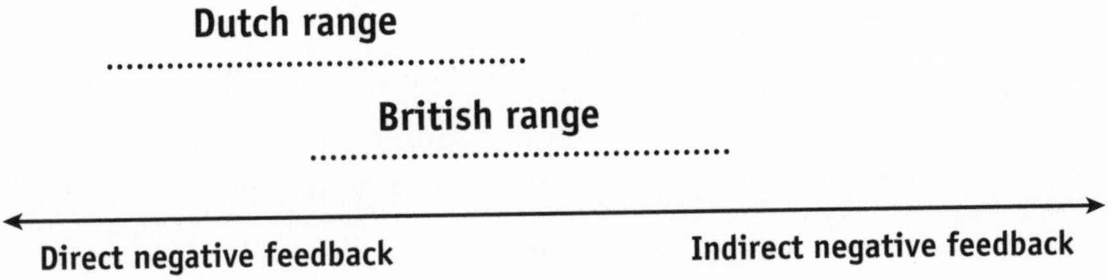

**Dutch range**

..........................................

**British range**

...................................

⟵————————————————————————⟶

Direct negative feedback                    Indirect negative feedback

be considered inappropriate, blunt, and offensive in the United Kingdom. The eight scales can help you understand such differences and evaluate individual choices within a broad cultural context.

## THE CRUCIAL PERSPECTIVE: CULTURAL RELATIVITY

Another crucial factor in understanding the meaning of the eight scales is the concept of cultural relativity. For an example, let's consider the location of Spain on the Trusting scale (Figure I.5), which positions cultures according to whether they build trust based on relationships or on experience of shared tasks.

Now ask yourself a simple question. Is Spain task-based or relationship-based? If you are like most people, you would answer that Spain is relationship-based. But this answer is subtly, yet crucially, wrong. The correct answer is that, if you come from France, the United Kingdom, Sweden, the United States, or any other culture

**FIGURE I.5.**

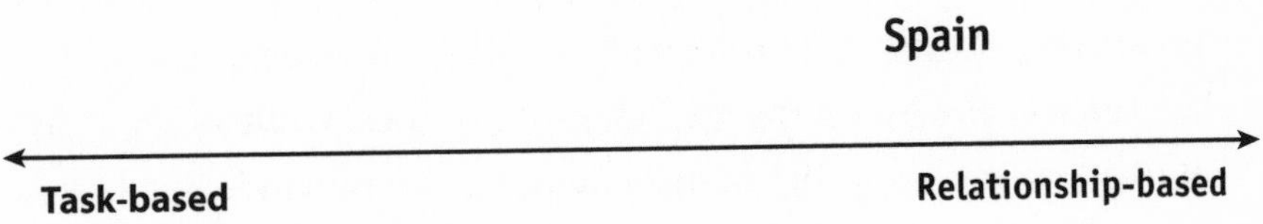

**Spain**

⟵————————————————————————⟶

Task-based                                 Relationship-based

that falls to the left of Spain on the scale, then Spain is relation-ship-based *in comparison to your own culture*. However, if you come from India, Saudi Arabia, Angola, or China, then Spain is very task-based indeed—again, in comparison to your own culture.

The point here is that, when examining how people from dif-ferent cultures relate to one another, what matters is not the abso-lute position of either culture on the scale but rather the relative position of the two cultures. It is this relative positioning that de-termines how people view one another.

For example, consider what happened when the British con-sulting group KPMG created several global teams to standardize the implementation of management software systems developed by enterprise software developer SAP. One global team was com-posed primarily of British and French consultants, and throughout their work the British complained that the French were disorga-nized, chaotic, and lacked punctuality. "They take so many tan-gents and side routes during the meeting, it's impossible to follow their line of thinking!" one British team member said.

On another team, made up of mainly Indians and French, the Indians complained that the French were rigid, inflexible, and ob-sessed with deadlines and structure to the point that they were un-able to adapt as the situation around them changed. "If you don't tell them weeks in advance what is going to happen in the meet-ing, in which order, it makes them very nervous," one Indian team member said.

Why such contradictory perceptions of the French team mem-bers? A quick glance at the Scheduling scale (Figure I.6) shows that the French fall *between* the British and the Indians, leading to op-posite perceptions from those two outlying perspectives.

When I described this experience to a group of Germans and British collaborating on another global team, one of the Germans

**FIGURE I.6.**

| Germany | UK | France | India |
|---|---|---|---|

Linear-time → Flexible-time

laughed. "That's very funny," he told us. "Because we Germans always complain that the British are disorganized, chaotic, and always late—exactly the complaint the British in your example lodged against the French." Note the relative positions of the Germans and British on the Scheduling scale.

So cultural relativity is the key to understanding the impact of culture on human interactions. If an executive wants to build and manage global teams that can work together successfully, he needs to understand not just how people from his own culture experience people from various international cultures, but also how those international cultures perceive *one another.*

## WHEN CULTURAL DIFFERENCES ARE INSIDE US

I recently had occasion to place a phone call to Cosimo Turroturro, who runs a speakers' association based in London. Simply on the basis of his name, I assumed before the call that he was Italian. But as soon as he spoke, starting sentences with the German "ja," it was clear that he was not.

Turroturro explained, "My mother was Serbian, my father was Italian, I was raised largely in Germany, although I have spent most of my adult life in the U.K. So you see, these cultural differences that you talk about, I don't need to speak to anyone else in order to experience them. I have all of these challenges right inside myself!"

I laughed, imagining Turroturro having breakfast alone and saying to himself in Italian, "Why do you have to be so blunt?" and responding to himself in German, "Me, blunt?! Why do *you* have to be so emotional?"

While most people spend most of their lives in their native lands, the scales in this book have an extra level of interest for those with more heterogeneous backgrounds. If you've lived in two or more countries or have parents from different countries, you may begin to notice how multiple cultures have helped to shape your personality. You may find that part of your personal style comes from the culture where you spent the first years of your life, another from the culture where you attended college and held your first job, another from your father's culture, and still another from your mother's culture. The following pages may not only help you become more effective as a businessperson; they may even help you understand yourself more fully than ever before.

## TASTING THE WATER YOU SWIM IN

Culture can be a sensitive topic. Speaking about a person's culture often provokes the same type of reaction as speaking about his mother. Most of us have a deep protective instinct for the culture we consider our own, and, though we may criticize it bitterly ourselves, we may become easily incensed if someone from outside the culture dares to do so. For this reason, I'm walking a minefield in this book.

I promise that all the situations I recount are drawn from the stories of real people working in real companies, though I've changed names, details, and circumstances to maintain anonymity. Nonetheless, you may find yourself reacting defensively when you hear what others have said about the culture you call your own: "It isn't true! My culture is not a bit like that!"

At the risk of pouring oil on the fire, allow me to repeat the familiar story of the two young fish who encounter an older fish swimming the opposite way. He nods at them and says, "Morning, boys, how's the water?"—which prompts one of the young fish to ask the other, "What the hell is water?"[1]

When you are in and of a culture—as fish are in and of water—it is often difficult or even impossible to *see* that culture. Often people who have spent their lives living in one culture see only regional and individual differences and therefore conclude, "My national culture does not have a clear character."

John Cleary, an engineer from the United States, explained this phenomenon during one of my courses for executives.

The first twenty-eight years of my life I lived in the smallish town of Madison, Wisconsin, but in my work I traveled across the U.S. weekly, since my team members were scattered across the country. The regional differences in the U.S. are strong. New York City feels entirely different than Athens, Georgia. So when I began working with foreigners who spoke of what it was like to work with "Americans," I saw that as a sign of ignorance. I would respond, "There is no American culture. The regions are different and within the regions every individual is different."

But then I moved to New Delhi, India. I began leading an Indian team and overseeing their collaboration with my former team in the U.S. I was very excited, thinking this would be an opportunity to learn about the Indian culture. After 16 months in New Delhi working with Indians and seeing this collaboration from the Indian viewpoint, I can report that I have learned a tremendous amount . . . about my own culture. As I view the American way of thinking and working and acting from this outside perspective, for the first time I see a clear, visible American culture. The culture of my country has a strong character that was totally invisible to me when I was in it and part of it.

When you hear the people quoted in this book complain, criticize, or gasp at your culture from their perspective, try not to take it as a personal affront. Instead, think of it as an opportunity to learn more not just about the unfamiliar cultures of this world but also about your own. Try seeing, feeling, and tasting the water you swim in the way a land animal might perceive it. You may find the experience fascinating—and mind-expanding.

\* \* \*

When I arrived back in my apartment in Paris after the session with the Bernards and Bo Chen, I thought back to the advice from Bo's mother. I Googled her words, "you have two eyes, two ears, and one mouth and you should use them accordingly," expecting the quotation to begin with "Confucius says" or at least "Bo Chen's mother says." No such luck. The ancient Greek philosopher Epictetus seems to have said something similar, but as far as I know he never lived in China.

That night, instead of dreaming about fruit disappearing from my shopping cart, I lay in bed thinking about why Bo Chen didn't speak up and why I kept speaking in the face of his silence, while—irony of ironies—I was running a session on cross-cultural effectiveness. I thought again about Mrs. Chen's advice and wished that I had followed her suggestion that morning.

Mrs. Chen's advice is sound, not just for Chinese children, but also for all of us who hope to improve our effectiveness working across cultural barriers. When interacting with someone from another culture, try to watch more, listen more, and speak less. Listen before you speak and learn before you act. Before picking up the phone to negotiate with your suppliers in China, your outsourcing team in India, your new boss in Brazil, or your clients in Russia, use all the available resources to understand how the cultural framework you are working with is different from your own—and only then react.

# 1

## Listening to the Air
### Communicating Across Cultures

When I arrived at my hotel in New Delhi, I was hot and, more important, hungry. Although I would spend that week conducting classes for a group of Indian executives at the swank five-star Oberoi hotel, the Indian business school hosting me put me up in a more modest and much smaller residence several miles away. Though quiet and clean, it looked like a big concrete box with windows, set back from the road and surrounded by a wall with a locked gate. This will be fine, I thought as I dropped my bag off in my room. Staying in a simple hotel just steps from the bustle of workaday New Delhi will make it that much easier for me to get the flavor of the city.

Lunch was at the top of my agenda. The very friendly young man behind the concierge desk jumped to attention when he saw me approaching. I asked about a good place to eat. "There is a great restaurant just to the left of the hotel. I recommend it highly," he told me. "It is called Swagat. You can't miss it."

It sounded perfect. I walked out to the road and looked to the left. The street was a whirlwind of colors, smells, and activities. I saw a grocery store, a cloth vendor, a family of five all piled onto one motor scooter, and a bunch of brown-speckled chickens peck-ing in the dust next to the sidewalk. No restaurant.

"You didn't find it?" the kind concierge asked in a puzzled tone as I re-entered the hotel. This time the young man explained, "Just walk out of the hotel, cross the street, and the restaurant will be on your left. It's next to the market. There is a sign. You can't miss it," he said again.

Well, apparently I could. I tried to do exactly as instructed, crossing the street immediately in front of the hotel and again looking to the left. As I saw no sign of the restaurant, I turned to the left and walked a while. It was a little confusing, as the street was jam-packed. After a minute or so, I came to a small side street full of people, food stalls, and women selling san-dals and saris. Was this the market the concierge mentioned? But after careful examination of what I felt to be all possible interpretations of "on your left," I began to wonder if I was be-ing filmed as a stunt for some type of reality TV show. I headed back to the hotel.

The concierge smiled kindly at me again, but I could tell he was thinking I really wasn't very smart. Scratching his head in bewilderment at my inability to find the obvious, he announced, "I will take you there." So we left the hotel, crossed the street, turned to the left, and then walked for nearly ten minutes, weav-ing our way through traffic on the bustling sidewalk and passing several side streets and countless heads of cattle on the way. At last, just beyond a large bank, perched quietly over a fruit store on the second floor of a yellow stucco building, I spotted a small sign that read SWAGAT.

As I thanked the concierge for his extreme kindness, I couldn't help wondering why he hadn't told me, "Cross the street, turn left, walk nine minutes, look for the big bank on the corner, and, when you see the big fruit store, look up to the second floor of the yellow stucco building for a sign with the restaurant's name."

And as this question floated through my mind, I could tell that the kindly concierge was wondering, "How will this poor, dim-witted woman possibly make it through the week?"

As my search for lunch in New Delhi suggests, the skills involved in being an effective communicator vary dramatically from one culture to another. In the United States and other Anglo-Saxon cultures, people are trained (mostly subconsciously) to communicate as literally and explicitly as possible. Good communication is all about clarity and explicitness, and accountability for accurate transmission of the message is placed firmly on the communicator: "If you don't understand, it's my fault."

By contrast, in many Asian cultures, including India, China, Japan, and Indonesia, messages are often conveyed implicitly, requiring the listener to read between the lines. Good communication is subtle, layered, and may depend on copious subtext, with responsibility for transmission of the message shared between the one sending the message and the one receiving it. The same applies to many African cultures, including those found in Kenya and Zimbabwe, and to a lesser degree Latin American cultures (such as Mexico, Brazil, and Argentina) and Latin European cultures (such as Spain, Italy, Portugal) including France.

The fact is that the hotel concierge provided all of the information necessary for someone from his own culture to find Swagat. An Indian living in the same Delhi cultural context would likely have figured out quickly where the restaurant was by the clues provided; she would have been eating her lunch while I was still wandering wearily around the streets.

My quest for the Swagat restaurant illustrates that being a good listener is just as important for effective communication as being a

good speaker. And both of these essential skills are equally vari-
able from one culture to another.

* * *

It was springtime in France, where I had been living several years,
when I was asked to give a presentation at a human resource conference in Paris sponsored by Owens Corning. A leading global
producer of residential building materials, Owens Corning is
headquartered in Toledo, Ohio—a good eleven-hour drive from
my home state of Minnesota, but still within the tribal boundaries
of my native midwestern American culture.

When I arrived at the conference, I found fifty human resource
directors assembled in a typical Parisian hotel space with high
ceilings and sunshine streaming through floor-to-ceiling windows. Thirty-eight of the participants were from Toledo; the rest
were from Europe and Asia, but all had been working for Owens
Corning for at least a decade. I took a seat in the back corner of the
room just as the presentation preceding mine was beginning.

The speaker would be David Brown, the company's CEO.
Relaxed and unimposing, wearing a blazer but no tie, David
strolled into the room wearing a warm smile and greeted several
of the attendees by their first name. But from the hush that descended when he stepped to the podium, it was obvious that this
group of HR directors considered him a celebrity. Brown spent
sixty intense minutes describing his vision of the company's future. He spoke in simple words, repeating key points and reinforc-
ing his messages with bullet-pointed slides. The group listened
carefully, asked a few respectful questions, and gave Brown an appreciative round of applause before he departed.

Now it was my turn. My job was to talk about the subject I
know best—cross-cultural management. I worked with the group

for an hour, explaining in detail the Communicating scale and its value as a tool for understanding how various cultures convey messages. As if to reinforce my theme, Kenji Takaki, a Japanese HR executive who had lived for two years in Toledo, raised his hand and offered this observation:

> In Japan, we implicitly learn, as we are growing up, to communicate between the lines and to listen between the lines when others are speaking. Communicating messages without saying them directly is a deep part of our culture, so deep that we do it without even realizing it. To give an example, every year in Japan there is a vote for the most popular new word. A few years ago, the word of the year was "KY." It stands for *kuuki yomenai*, which means "one who cannot read the air"—in other words, a person sorely lacking the ability to read between the lines. In Japan if you can't read the air, you are not a good listener.

At this point one of the Americans broke in, "What do you mean, 'read the air'?"

Takaki explained, "If I am in a meeting in Japan and one person is implicitly communicating disagreement or discomfort, we should be able to read the atmosphere to pick up on that discomfort. If someone else doesn't pick up the message we say, 'He is a KY guy!'"

The American chuckled, "I guess that means we Americans are all KY guys!" Takaki offered no comment, which I read as an indication that he agreed. Then Takaki continued:

> When Mr. Brown was giving his presentation, I was working hard to listen with all of my senses—to make sure I was picking up all of the messages that he was trying to pass. But now as I am

listening to Erin I am asking myself: Is it possible there was no meaning beyond Mr. Brown's very simple words? And with all of you in this very room, whom I have worked with for so many years, when I read the air during our discussions, am I picking up messages you had not intended to pass?

This was a very astute question—and a very disturbing one. The group fell silent, with a few jaws hanging slightly agape, as Takaki quietly read the air.

*  *  *

The contrasting styles of communication represented by the managers from Toledo and their colleague from Japan are often referred to as *low-context* and *high-context*, respectively.

In order to understand some of the implications, suppose you are having a discussion with Sally, a business colleague, and you both come from a culture that prefers low-context communication. People from such cultures are conditioned from childhood to assume a low level of shared context—that is, few shared reference points and comparatively little implicit knowledge linking speaker and listener.

Under these circumstances, it's highly likely that, while speaking with Sally, you will explicitly spell out your ideas, providing all the background knowledge and details necessary to understand your message. In low-context cultures, effective communication must be simple, clear, and explicit in order to effectively pass the message, and most communicators will obey this requirement, usually without being fully conscious of it. The United States is the lowest-context culture in the world, followed by Canada and Australia, the Netherlands and Germany, and the United Kingdom.

Though cultural norms are transmitted from one generation to the next through means that are generally indirect and subliminal, you may remember receiving some deliberate lessons concerning appropriate ways to communicate. I certainly received such lessons as a child growing up in the United States. My third-grade teacher, Mary Jane, a tall, thin woman with tightly curled hair, used to coach us during our Monday morning circle meetings using the motto, "Say what you mean and mean what you say." When I was sixteen, I took an elective class at Minneapolis South High School on giving effective presentations. This is where I learned the traditional American rule for successfully transferring a powerful message to an audience: "Tell them what you are going to tell them, then tell them, then tell them what you've told them." This is the philosophy of low-context communication in a nutshell.

I received lessons in low-context communication at home, too. Like many siblings, my older brother and I argued constantly. In an effort to reduce our squabbling, Mom used to coach us in active listening: You speak to me as clearly and explicitly as possible. Then I'll repeat what I understood you to say as clearly and explicitly as I can. The technique is designed to help people quickly identify and correct misunderstandings, thereby reducing (if not eliminating) one common cause of needless, pointless debate.

Childhood lessons like these imbued me with the assumption that being explicit is simply good communication. But, as Takaki explained, good communication in a high-context culture like Japan is very different. In Japan as in India, China, and many other countries, people learn a very different style of communication as children—one that depends on unconscious assumptions about common reference points and shared knowledge.

For example, let's say that you and a business colleague named Maryam both come from a high-context culture like Iran. Imagine that Maryam has traveled to your home for a visit and arrived via a late-evening train at 10:00 p.m. If you ask Maryam whether she would like to eat something before going to bed, when Maryam responds with a polite "No, thank you," your response will be to ask her two more times. Only if she responds "No, thank you" three times will you accept "No" as her real answer.

The explanation lies in shared assumptions that every polite Iranian understands. Both you and Maryam know that a well-mannered person will not accept food the first time it is offered, no matter how hungry she may be. Thus, if you don't ask her a second or third time, Maryam may go to bed suffering from hunger pains, while you feel sorry that she hasn't tasted the chicken salad you'd prepared especially for her.

In a high-context culture like Iran, it's not necessary—indeed, it's often inappropriate—to spell out certain messages too explicitly. If Maryam replied to your first offer of food, "Yes, please serve me a big portion of whatever you have, because I am dying of hunger!" this response would be considered inelegant and perhaps quite rude. Fortunately, shared assumptions learned from childhood make such bluntness unnecessary. You and Maryam both know that "No, thank you" likely means, "Please ask me again because I am famished."

Remember my confusing encounter with the concierge in New Delhi? If I had been an Indian from Delhi with the shared cultural understanding of how to interpret implicit messages, I would have been better able to interpret the concierge's directions. Lacking those assumptions left me bewildered and unable to find my way to the restaurant.

## THE INTERPLAY OF LANGUAGE AND HISTORY

Languages reflect the communication styles of the cultures that use those languages. For example, Japanese and Hindi (as spoken in New Delhi) are both high-context languages, in which a relatively high percentage of words can be interpreted multiple ways based on how and when they are used. In Japanese, for instance, the word "ashi" means both "leg" and "foot," depending on context. Japanese also possesses countless homonyms, of which there are only a few in English ("dear" and "deer," for example). In Hindi the word "kal" means both tomorrow and yesterday. You have to hear the whole sentence to understand in which context it has been used. For this reason, when speaking Japanese or Hindi, you really do have to "read the air" to understand the message.

I work in English and also in French, a much higher-context language than English. For one thing, there are seven times more words in English than in French (500,000 versus 70,000), which suggests that French relies on contextual clues to resolve semantic ambiguities to a greater extent than English. Many words in French have multiple possible meanings—for example, *ennuyé* can mean either "bored" or "bothered" depending on the context in which it's used—which means that the listener is responsible for discerning the intention of the speaker.

The French language contains a number of idioms that specifically refer to high-context communication. One is *sous-entendu*, literally meaning "under the heard." To use a *sous-entendu* basically means to say something without saying it. For example, if a man says to his wife, "There are a lot of calories in that toffee ice cream you bought," his *sous-entendu* may be "You have gained some weight, so don't eat this ice cream." He has not explicitly said that she is getting fat, but when he sees her reach down to throw a shoe at him, he will know that she picked up his *sous-entendu*.

I once asked a French client, who was complaining about an incompetent team leader, whether he had described the problem to his boss. The client responded. "Well, yes, but it was a *sous-entendu*. I made it known so that he could see it if he wanted to see it." The same expressions exist in Spanish (*sobrentendido*) and Portuguese (*subentendido*) and although less common, they are used in much the same way.

A similar French expression refers to saying something at the *deuxième degré* (literally, "the second degree"). I may say one thing explicitly—my first-degree message—but the statement may have an unspoken subtext which is the second-degree meaning.

The use of second-degree messages is a feature of French literature. Consider the seventeenth-century writer Jean de La Fontaine. At the first degree, he wrote simple children's tales, but if you understand the contemporary context within which the stories were written, you may pick up his second degree of meaning—a political message for adults. For example, La Fontaine's famous fable of the grasshopper and the ant conveys a straightforward moral that most children understand: It's important to economize to prepare for difficult times. But only sophisticated adult readers of his own day recognized La Fontaine's second-degree message—that King Louis XIV should stop spending so much money on rerouting the Eure River to supply water to the Versailles fountains.

In France, a good business communicator will use second-degree communication in everyday life. While giving a presentation, a manager may say one thing that has an explicit meaning everyone understands. But those who have some shared context may also receive a second-degree message that is the *real* intended meaning.

English, then, is a lower-context language than the Romance languages descended from Latin (French, Spanish, Italian, and Portuguese), while the Romance languages are lower context than most Asian languages. However, a look at the Communicating scale and its ranking of cultures from most explicit to most implicit shows that language is not the whole story (see Figure 1.1).

The United States is the lowest-context culture in the world, and all Anglo-Saxon cultures fall on the left-hand side of the scale, with the United Kingdom as the highest-context culture of the Anglo-Saxon cluster. All the countries that speak Romance languages, including European countries like Italy, Spain, and France, and Latin American countries like Mexico, Brazil, and Argentina, fall to the middle right of the scale. Brazil is the lowest-context culture in this cluster. Many African and Asian countries fall even further right. Japan has the distinction of being the highest-context culture in the world.

As you can see, language only gives a partial indicator as to where a culture will fall on the Communicating scale. The gap

### FIGURE 1.1. COMMUNICATING

| US | Netherlands | | Finland | | | Spain | Italy | Singapore | Iran | China | Japan |
| | Australia | Germany | Denmark | Poland | Brazil | Mexico | France | | India | Kenya | Korea |
| | Canada | | UK | | | Argentina | Peru | Russia | | Saudi | Indonesia |
| | | | | | | | | | | Arabia | |

← ——————————————————————————————————————————— →

**Low-Context**                                                      **High-Context**

................................................................................................................

**Low-Context**   Good communication is precise, simple, and clear. Messages are expressed and understood at face falue. Repetition is appreciated if it helps clarify the communication.

**High-Context**   Good communication is sophisticated, nuanced, and layered. Messages are both spoken and read between the lines. Messages are often implied but not plainly expressed.

between the United States and the United Kingdom, both Anglo-Saxon countries, is quite large, as is the gap between Brazil and Peru, both Romance-language countries.

Beyond language, the history of a country strongly impacts its position on the Communicating scale. For an example, just think for a minute about the histories of the two bookend countries on the scale, the United States and Japan.

High-context cultures tend to have a long shared history. Usually they are relationship-oriented societies where networks of connections are passed on from generation to generation, generating more shared context among community members. Japan is an island society with a homogeneous population and thousands of years of shared history, during a significant portion of which Japan was closed off from the rest of the world. Over these thousands of years, people became particularly skilled at picking up each other's messages—reading the air, as Takaki said.

By contrast, the United States, a country with a mere few hundred years of shared history, has been shaped by enormous inflows of immigrants from various countries around the world, all with different histories, different languages, and different backgrounds. Because they had little shared context, Americans learned quickly that if they wanted to pass a message, they had to make it as explicit and clear as possible, with little room for ambiguity and misunderstanding.

So within each language cluster you may notice a pattern (see Figure 1.2). First, countries are clustered by language type. On the left, you see the Anglo-Saxon cluster, followed by the Romance language cluster, and finally, furthest to the right, is a cluster of countries speaking Asian languages. Then within each cluster, you might notice how length of history and level of homogeneity impact the

### FIGURE 1.2. **COMMUNICATING**

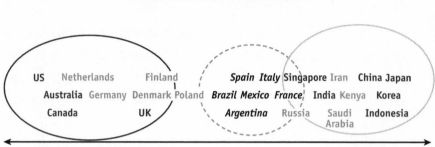

Low-context                                                    High-context

communication style. For example, within the Anglo-Saxon cluster, the United States has the most linguistic and cultural diversity and the shortest shared history. This helps to explain why the United States is the lowest-context of the Anglo-Saxon cultures. In the Romance cluster, Brazil has the most diversity and is the lowest-context culture. The same pattern holds with Asia, where the lower-context countries like Singapore and India have the most linguistic and cultural diversity.

The American anthropologist Edward Hall, who originally developed the concept of low- and high-context communication while working on Native American reservations in the 1930s, often used the analogy of marriage to describe the differences between high- and low-context communication. Imagine what happens when two people are married for fifty or sixty years. Having shared the same context for so long, they can gather enormous amounts of information just by looking at each other's faces or gestures. Newlyweds, however, need to state their messages explicitly and repeat them frequently to ensure they are received accurately.[1] The comparison to countries with longer or shorter shared histories is obvious.

## WHAT MAKES A GOOD COMMUNICATOR?

In everyday life, we all communicate explicitly sometimes, while passing messages between the lines in other situations. But when you say someone is "a good communicator," what exactly do you mean? The way you answer this question suggests where you fall on the scale.

A Dutch executive in one of my classes noticed his country's low-context positioning on the scale and protested, "We speak between the lines in the Netherlands, too." But when asked whether a businessman who communicates between the lines frequently would be considered a good or a bad communicator, he didn't have to think long. "Bad. That's the difference between us and the French," he said. "In the Netherlands, if you don't say it straight, we don't think you are trustworthy."

If you're from a low-context culture, you may perceive a high-context communicator as secretive, lacking transparency, or unable to communicate effectively. Lou Edmondson, an American vice president for sales at Kraft who travels around the world negotiating deals with suppliers in Asia and Eastern Europe, put it starkly: "I have always believed that people say what they mean and mean what they say—and if they don't, well, then, they are lying."

On the other hand, if you're from a high-context culture, you might perceive a low-context communicator as inappropriately stating the obvious ("You didn't have to say it! We all understood!"), or even as condescending and patronizing ("You talk to us like we are children!"). Although I have lived and worked outside the United States for many years, low-context communication is still my natural style. I'm embarrassed to admit that I have been subjected to both of these accusations more than once by my European colleagues.

A few years ago, a New York–based financial institution that I'd worked with previously asked me to do a cultural audit of their organization. Since corporate culture is not my specialty and I lacked the time necessary to do this project justice, I approached an Italian colleague whom I'll call Paolo about collaborating with me.

Paolo greeted me cheerfully when we met in his office. Twenty-five years my senior, Paolo has a well-earned reputation as an exceptional researcher and writer. He gave me a copy of his newest book and listened with interest as I described the collaboration opportunity. I started by explaining that my work, family, and writing commitments provided very little time for this project. Paolo nodded, and then the two of us explored the opportunity in more depth, discussing the client company and the specific issues that needed to be addressed. Still feeling a bit anxious about my time limitations, I repeated that Paolo would need to do 80 percent of the work (and would of course receive 80 percent of the compensation). Then we returned to exploring the needs of the client and possible approaches, but after a few more minutes, I once again slipped in my concern about time.

Paolo laughed impatiently: "Erin, I am not a child. I was not born yesterday. I understand very well what your point is." I felt myself blushing with embarrassment. Paolo is quite used to reading subtle messages; he had grasped my not-so-subtle point the *first* time. I apologized, wondering whether Paolo often reacted this way when speaking with the dozens of American faculty members at INSEAD who clarify and repeat themselves endlessly.

The moral of the story is clear: You may be considered a top-flight communicator in your home culture, but what works at home may not work so well with people from other cultures.

One interesting quirk is that in high-context cultures, the more educated and sophisticated you are, the greater your ability to both speak and listen with an understanding of implicit, layered messages. By contrast, in low-context cultures, the most educated and sophisticated business people are those who communicate in a clear, explicit way. The result is that the chairman of a French or Japanese company is likely to be a lot more high-context than those who work on the shop floor of the same company, while the chairman of an American or Australian organization is likely to be more low-context than those with entry-level jobs in the same organization. In this respect, education tends to move individuals toward a more extreme version of the dominant cultural tendency.

## IT'S ALL RELATIVE

As we've noted, when considering the impact of cultural differences on your dealings with other people, what matters is not so much the absolute positioning of a person's culture on a particular scale, but rather their *relative* positioning in comparison to you. The examples that follow illustrate how this principle applies to the Communicating scale.

Both Americans and British fall toward the low-context end of the Communicating scale. But the British speak more between the lines than Americans do, a tendency particularly apparent with British high-context humor. Many British people are fond of delivering ironic or sarcastic jokes with a completely deadpan face. Unfortunately, this kind of humor is lost on many Americans; they may *suspect* the British person is joking but they don't dare laugh, just in case he is not.

As a result, the British often say that Americans "don't understand irony." However, a more precise explanation is that Americans are simply more low-context than the British. So when Americans make a joke, especially in a professional setting, they are likely to indicate clearly through explicit verbal or physical cues, "This is a joke," something totally unnecessary when one British person is speaking to another. In their higher-context culture, if you have to tell us it was a joke, then it wasn't worth the breath you used to tell it.

Alastair Murray, a British manager living in Dubai, offers this example:

I was participating in a long-distance bike race across the UAE desert with hundreds of participants. In order to be collegial, I took a turn riding in front of another biker in order to break the headwind for him and help him save a little energy. A stranger had recently done the same for me.

A little later the biker peddled up next to me and said in a thick American accent, "Thanks very much for your help!"

I replied, "Oh, sure! But I wouldn't have done it if I'd known you were American."

To someone British it would have been clear that this was a joke, and even a sort of gentle reaching-out of friendliness. But as I delivered it straight-faced and with a serious voice, the American didn't seem to get it. He rode next to me in silence, beginning to pull slightly to the side.

So then I thought about how often Americans say "just kidding" after a joke. So I gave it a go. I told him, "Oh, hey, just kidding!"

And he responded, "Oh! All right! Ha ha! That was a good one. Where are you from?"

Oh, gosh, I thought. . . . these literal Americans!

The British may be more high-context than Americans—particularly where humor is concerned—but in comparison with Latin Europeans such as Spain and Italy and including the French they are very low-context.

I once worked with Stuart Shuttleworth, the CEO, owner, and founder of a small British investment firm that had grown over thirty years from a one-man shop into a company with one hundred employees. Two years earlier, he had begun expanding the business internationally. Shuttleworth explained to me the cultural quandaries this expansion had created for him:

> Every day, as I see how my new counterparts work in Spain, France, and Italy, I am asking myself if it is possible that what is obvious common sense to me may not be common sense in those environments. Take, for example, the simple process of recapping a meeting. In the U.K., it is common sense that at the end of a meeting you should verbally recap what has been decided, which is most frequently followed by a written recap, including individual action items, which we send out to all meeting participants. Clarification, clarification, clarification—in the U.K. this is simply good business practice.
>
> I attended a meeting the other day in Paris with a group of my France-based employees and one of our Parisian clients. As the meeting was clearly winding down, I awaited the final "Here's what we've decided" recap of the meeting. Instead, one of the clients announced dramatically "Et voilà!" [There it is!] as if everything had been made clear. The others all stood up patting

one another on the back and shaking hands, stating words of appreciation and future collaboration.

I couldn't help but wonder, "But voilà what?" It seems that my French colleagues simply *know* what has been decided and who should do what without going through all of the levels of clarification that we are used to in the U.K.

Shuttleworth was also confused by the e-mail etiquette he encountered:

In the U.K., as in the U.S., if you send someone an e-mail and that person doesn't have the answer at their fingertips, both common sense and etiquette call for the receiver to respond within 24 hours saying something like, "I got your message and will get back to you on Wednesday." In other words, even if you have nothing to say, you should spell out explicitly in a low-context way when you *will* have something to say. Lack of explicit communication signifies something negative.

Now, I send an e-mail to our Spanish supplier—who I know does high-quality and on-time work and has a very good level of English—and I may not hear back from him or any of his colleagues for three or four days. I am biting my nails assuming all sorts of problems with my request that prevent a speedy reply . . . either that or the entire staff has fallen ill or the building has burned down so that no one can read their e-mails.

And then three days later, I receive an e-mail telling me that they have done exactly as requested and everything is under control. Why couldn't they have said that in the first place?!

French, Spanish, and Italian are markedly more high-context than Anglo-Saxon cultures. But the cultures of Asia are even more high-context than any in Europe. As the center of the business world tilts towards China, understanding the communication patterns typical of Chinese culture becomes increasingly critical.

Elisabeth Shen is a consultant who splits her time between Shanghai and Paris, helping Europeans work effectively with the Chinese. This can be quite challenging, since, as Shen observes, "China is a huge country with strong regional differences. In many ways it is difficult to categorize Chinese business culture, given its wide generational gaps and differences between private and public sectors." However, it's safe to say that Chinese culture in general is very high-context in comparison with the cultures of the West. Shen explains:

> When Chinese vaguely express an idea or an opinion, the real message is often just implied. They expect their conversational partner to be highly involved and to take an active role in deciphering messages, as well as in mutually creating meaning. In Chinese culture, *pang qiao ce ji* [beating around the bush] is a style that nurtures an implicit understanding. In Chinese culture, children are taught not to just hear the explicit words but also to focus on *how* something is said, and on what is *not* said.

I collaborated with Shen to conduct interviews with dozens of European managers from various business sectors who had spent significant portions of their careers in different regions of China. They had varying opinions on how to succeed in a Chinese environment. In one of these interviews, Pablo Díaz, a Spanish executive who worked in China for a Chinese textile company for fifteen years, remarked, "In China, the message up front is not necessarily the real message. My Chinese colleagues would drop hints, and I wouldn't pick them up. Later, when thinking it over, I would realize I had missed something important." Díaz recounts a discussion he had with a Chinese employee which went something like this:

> **MR. DÍAZ:** It looks like some of us are going to have to be here on Sunday to host the client visit.
> **MR. CHEN:** I see.
> **MR. DÍAZ:** Can you join us on Sunday?
> **MR. CHEN:** Yes, I think so.
> **MR. DÍAZ:** That would be a great help.
> **MR. CHEN:** Yes, Sunday is an important day.
> **MR. DÍAZ:** In what way?
> **MR. CHEN:** It's my daughter's birthday.
> **MR. DÍAZ:** How nice. I hope you all enjoy it.
> **MR. CHEN:** Thank you. I appreciate your understanding.[2]

Díaz laughs about the situation now. "I was quite certain he had said he was coming," Díaz says. "And Mr. Chen was quite certain he had communicated that he absolutely could not come because he was going to be celebrating his daughter's birthday with his family."

Díaz has learned from experience how to avoid falling into these communication snafus:

> If I'm not 100 percent sure what I heard, shrugging my shoulders and leaving with the message that I sort of think I heard is not a good strategy. If I am not sure, I have to take the responsibility to ask for clarification. Sometimes I have to ask three or four times, and although that can be a little embarrassing for both me and my colleague, it is not as embarrassing as having a production line set and ready and waiting for Mr. Chen, who is contentedly singing happy birthday somewhere else.

## STRATÉGIES FOR WORKING WITH PEOPLE FROM
## HIGHER-CONTEXT CULTURES

As you can see, communicating across cultures can be fraught with invisible difficulties. Whether you consider yourself a low-context or high-context communicator, it's quite likely you will one day find yourself working with a colleague, client, or partner positioned further to the right on the scale. So being an agile communicator, able to move adroitly in either direction, is a valuable skill for anyone in business.

When considering strategies for improving your effectiveness, one crucial principle to remember is that communicating is not just about speaking but also listening. Pablo Díaz has learned this from experience. "It isn't just that my Chinese employees speak between the lines," he says. "They are also always trying to find out what is behind a comment. This type of listening is not natural for Westerners, who take everything at face value."

So when you work with higher-context colleagues, practice listening more carefully. "The best advice I can give," Díaz says, "is to learn to listen to what is *meant* instead of what is said. This means reflecting more, asking more clarifying questions, and making an effort to be more receptive to body language cues." By searching for implicit cues, you can begin to "read the air" a little more accurately.

Think back to the dialogue between Mr. Chen and Mr. Díaz above. In this dialogue, Mr. Chen says "yes," but he simultaneously indicates that the real answer is "no." Saying "no" between the lines is common throughout Asia, including China, Japan, and Korea, and especially when speaking to a boss or a client. If you work with a supplier or a team member from one of these countries, you'll discover that "no" can come in many guises. A question like "Can you complete this project by next week?" may be greeted by a sharp sucking-in of breath or a noncommittal answer: "It will be very difficult, but I'll do my best," "We'll think about it," or "It will be hard for these reasons, but let me consider it."

With practice, you can learn to read the "no" between the lines. For verification, ask open-ended questions rather than backing the person into a corner that requires a yes or no response. For example, Mr. Díaz could have asked an open-ended clarifying question such as, "How difficult would it be for you to get away from the party to come to work for a few hours?" With persistence, more information will emerge.

"It is important not to form opinions too quickly," Díaz suggests, "to listen more, speak less, and then clarify when you are not sure if you understood. You might need to work through another local person in order to get the message deciphered. But if you feel confused, work to get all the information you need to pick up the intended message." One of the biggest mistakes lower-context managers make is assuming that the other individual is *purposely* omitting information or *unable* to communicate explicitly. Most often, the higher-context person is simply communicating in the style to which he is accustomed, with no thought of confusing or misleading you. Simply asking for clarification can work wonders. After a while, you may find you don't have to ask so many times for clarity, as your counterpart also learns to adapt to you.

If you are the one sending the message, you may find there is less need to repeat yourself endlessly when speaking with high-context colleagues who listen between the lines. Before repeating yourself, stop talking. Wait to learn whether saying it once is enough. You can always come back to the topic later if you're not sure whether the message got through.

When you find yourself stymied or frustrated by misunderstanding, self-deprecation, laughing at yourself, and using positive words to describe the other culture are always good options. For example, when I was searching for the Swagat restaurant in New Delhi, I could have mentioned to the concierge that I come from a country with small towns, few people, and lots of signposts: "Indian people have a knack for finding things that I do not have. Please be so kind as to draw me a map marking every landmark or street I will see on the way to the restaurant." Or I might have said, "I am really bad at finding things, and this city is totally new to me. Could you please make me a simple drawing that a young child could read, marking exactly what I will see on each step of my way and each road I will cross? If you could include exactly how many minutes it will take me to walk for each part of the journey, that will help, as I do have a poor sense of direction." Self-deprecation allows you to accept the blame for being unable to get the message and then ask for assistance.

## STRATEGIES FOR WORKING WITH PEOPLE FROM LOWER-CONTEXT CULTURES

Having consulted frequently with Western companies outsourcing to India, I was quite used to hearing the comments, "When I explained what needed to be done to my Indian team, there were no questions. Later, I realized they hadn't understood my instructions. Why didn't they ask for clarification?"

Later, when the Indian Institute of Planning and Management organized a multiple-city tour where I was to work with executives in four Indian cities, I experienced more of this high-context communication. As I prepared for the trip, I frequently found myself

communicating by both phone and e-mail with the university organizers, asking questions like, "Who exactly will be attending my
sessions? What kinds of international experience do they have?
Why are they interested in hearing from me? What sorts of questions should I anticipate?" Unfortunately, the responses I received
were so high-context that I often felt more confused than before I
asked. The names, backgrounds, and specific business needs of the
attendees remained vague and unknown to me until I arrived in
the classroom.

These experiences prepared me well for a question that one of
the class participants asked me during a lunch break. "Madam,"
he said politely, "what you have taught us this morning is very
important to my daily job. I have never traveled outside India, but
I work every day by phone and e-mail with American, Australian,
and British clients. What is the best way to build trust with these
colleagues and customers?"

Thinking back to my difficulties of a few weeks earlier as well
as previous experience working with Western companies outsourcing to India, I had a ready response:

> Be as transparent, clear, and specific as possible. Explain ex-
> actly why you are calling. Assert your opinions transparently.
> Show all of your cards up front. At the end of the phone call,
> recap all the key points again, or send an e-mail repeating
> these points straight afterwards. If you are ever not 100 per-
> cent sure what you have been asked to do, don't read between
> the lines but state clearly that you don't understand and ask
> for clarification. And sometimes it would be better to not be
> quite so polite, as it gives the impression of vagueness or
> uncertainty.

With a little effort and practice, someone from a higher-context environment can learn to work and communicate in a lower-context way. Focus on recognizing when you are expecting the other person to read your intended message between the lines and get in the habit of conveying it more explicitly. Start the conversation by stating the main idea, make your points clearly, and at the end of the discussion recap what has been decided and what will happen next. If you're not sure whether your ideas have been absorbed, then feel free to ask, "Am I clear enough?" Follow up with an e-mail clarifying anything that might still be a bit vague and stating the main conclusions in writing.

I've come across people from high-context cultures who have gotten so good at switching their styles that they become as low-context as the American on the other end of the phone line.

## STRATEGIES FOR MULTICULTURAL COLLABORATIONS

What if you have a blend of many cultures all on one team—Americans who recap incessantly and nail everything down in writing, Japanese who read the air, French who speak at the second degree, British who love to use deadpan irony as a form of humor, and Chinese who learn as young children to beat around the bush? Where do you suppose the greatest likelihood of misunderstanding will arise? Consider three options:

A.  One low-context person communicating with someone
    from another low-context culture (for example,
    a Dutchman communicating with a Canadian)
B.  A high-context person communicating with a
    low-context person (for example, a Spaniard
    communicating with a Dutchman)

C.  One high-context person communicating with someone
     from another high-context culture (for example. a
     person from China communicating with a Brazilian).

Many people assume that the answer is choice B—a low-context/high-context conversation. The correct answer is choice C. On a multicultural team, most misunderstanding takes place between people who come from two high-context cultures with entirely different roots, such as the Brazilians communicating with the Chinese.

High-context communication works beautifully when we are from the same culture and interpret cultural cues the same way. When two Japanese people communicate, the shared contextual understanding makes it easy for them to read the air. Time is saved (no need to repeat an idea three times), relationships are maintained (no need to tell you a direct "no" when I can hint at it and you can pick up the message), and group harmony is preserved. But when team members come from different cultures, high-context communication breaks down. The speaker may be passing a message between the lines, and the listener may be actively focused on scanning for meaning. But because the two individuals come from completely different cultural contexts, the message received is different from the message sent, and the likelihood of misunderstanding multiplies.

Fortunately, if you are leading a multicultural team, there's no need to count the number of team members from the left and right hand of the scale and multiply by the number of members to figure out what to do. There is just one easy strategy to remember: *Multicultural teams need low-context processes.*

Pedro Galvez, a Mexican manager at Johnson and Johnson, attended my weeklong program on managing global virtual teams. He found himself managing a team that included both Mexicans and Saudi Arabians—representatives of two very different high-context cultures. Galvez recalls:

> The Saudis had a different way of passing and interpreting messages from the Mexicans, and we quickly began misunderstanding one another. Following a miscommunication between one of my Mexican team members and his Saudi colleague, I spoke with each of them about what had happened. The Mexican told me, "I made it known, so he could see it if he wanted to see it." I could see that with this kind of misunderstanding occurring, we might be headed for serious trouble.
>
> After that incident, I brought the team together and we set ground rules. I spoke about the likelihood of misunderstanding given our different languages, our different cultural backgrounds, and the fact that both of our cultures have a tendency to communicate implicitly and pass messages between the lines. I asked the group to come up with solutions for minimizing misunderstanding, and in small groups they developed a process for how we would work together.

The list of ground rules developed by Galvez's group was simple but effective. Three levels of verification would take place at the end of any meeting:

- One person would recap the key points orally, with the task rotating from one team member to another.
- Each person would summarize orally what he would do next.
- One person would send out a written recap, again on a rotating basis.

A similar system of explicit recaps and summaries would be used after one-on-one conversations or phone calls. The purpose— to catch and correct any misunderstandings or confusions.

If you have members from more than one high-context culture on your team, lay out the issue and have the team develop their own solutions, as Pedro did. Don't wait until problems arise. The best moment to develop the processes is when the team is forming, *before* miscommunication takes place.

And one more point. Galvez's team added to their list of rules the following statement: "This is our team culture, which we have explicitly agreed on and all feel comfortable with." Galvez knew that making everyone comfortable with the explicit, written agreement was both important and challenging. Putting things in writing may signify a lack of trust in some high-context cultures. So when he asked the group to begin putting things in writing, he made sure to lay some groundwork.

## WHEN SHOULD YOU PUT IT IN WRITING?

The more low-context the culture, the more people have a tendency to put everything in writing. "That was a fine meeting—I'll send out a written recap." "Thanks for the phone call—I'll send you an e-mail listing the next steps." "You're hired—here's your written job description and a formal offer letter." This explains why, compared with European and Asian companies, American businesses tend to have more:

- Organizational charts (showing on paper who works for whom)
- Titles (describing exactly who is at what level)

- Written objectives (explaining who is responsible for accomplishing what)
- Performance appraisals (stating in writing how each person is doing)

By contrast, many high-context cultures—particularly those of Asia and Africa—have a strong oral tradition in which written documentation is considered less necessary. The tendency to put everything in writing, which is a mark of professionalism and transparency in a low-context culture, may suggest to high-context colleagues that you don't trust them to follow through on their verbal commitments.

"This happened to me!" Bethari Syamsudin, an Indonesian manager working for the multinational automotive supplier Valeo, told me. "My boss is German, but my team is all Indonesian. In my culture, if we have a strong relationship and come to a spoken agreement, that is enough for me. So if you get off the phone and send me an e-mail recapping in writing everything we have just decided, that would be a clear sign to me that you don't trust me."

Bethari was willing to adapt her style in deference to the wishes of her German superior. She recalls:

My boss asked me to do what I could to make the communication more transparent in our office. He complained that he often didn't know what decisions had been made and wanted a higher level of clarity. So he asked me to send a written recap of our weekly Bangkok team meeting to him and all participants in order to boost the clarity.

I will never forget the reaction of my Indonesian team when I sent out the first recap putting all of them on copy. My good friend and colleague called two minutes after the recap was sent out and said, "Don't you trust me, Bethari? I told you I would do it in the meeting. You know I am good on my word." She thought I was being "political"—which is what we often say about the Europeans. I was caught between the culture of my boss and the culture of my staff.

At the next team meeting, Bethari explained carefully to the team why she was putting everything in writing and asked for their indulgence. "It was that easy," she says. "Once people understood I was asking for a written recap because the big boss requested it, they were fine with that. And, as I explained that this was a very natural way to work in Germany, they were doubly fine with it. If I ever need my staff to behave in a non-Indonesian way, I now start by explaining the cultural difference. If I don't, the negative reactions fly."

If you work with a team that has both low-context and high-context members, follow Bethari's lead. Putting it in writing reduces confusion and saves time for multi-cultural teams. But make sure to explain up front why you are doing it.

\* \* \*

Now, let's return to my adventures in New Delhi, from the beginning of the chapter. After a delicious lunch of palak paneer I left the Swagat restaurant and returned to the hotel. The same friendly concierge smiled warmly as I approached. After telling him how much I enjoyed my lunch I explained that I hoped to visit the Qutab Minar ancient ruins that afternoon. He looked a little nervous, perhaps weary after my difficulty finding the restaurant just down the street. "Could you please map out for me step-by-step exactly what I need to do at every moment in order to find the ruins? As you have witnessed I'm not used to such a busy city."

Perhaps now certain of my inability to maneuver anywhere, let alone to the busy ruins in the middle of town, he said to me, "Don't worry Madam. I will organize everything. We have a driver who will take you right to the entrance and pick you up in the same spot. In the meantime I will provide you with a map with the address of the hotel clearly marked and every landmark between here and the ruins. And please take this card with my phone number on it. If you get lost and can't find the driver I will come and find you myself." And thus began a marvelous afternoon in New Delhi.

# 2

## The Many Faces of Polite

Evaluating Performance and
Providing Negative Feedback

S abine Dulac, the finance director we met in the introduction, leaned back in her chair and let out a frustrated sigh.
Managing Americans was proving much more difficult than she
could have ever imagined. Her new American boss, Jake Webber,
had reported to Dulac that several of her team members had complained bitterly following their first round of performance reviews
with Dulac. They felt she'd been brutal and unfair in her feedback,
focusing heavily on the negative points and hardly mentioning all
their hard work and accomplishments.

Dulac was dumbfounded. The way she had provided feedback
was the same style she'd used successfully with dozens of French
employees with great success. Where were these complaints coming from?

Dulac was particularly confused because she'd expected
American culture to be very direct. "In France, we frequently
talk about how direct and explicit Americans are. Subtle? Hardly.
Sophisticated? Not at all. But transparent and direct—we all know
this to be true."

In this chapter, we'll build on the Communicating scale from the last chapter while adding an important twist. Some cultures that are low-context and explicit may be cryptically indirect with negative criticism, while other cultures that speak between the lines may be explicit, straight talkers when telling you what you did wrong. As we will see, the French and the Americans are not the only cultures that swap places on the Communicating and Evaluating scales.

The Evaluating scale will provide you with important insights into how to give effective performance appraisals and negative feedback in different parts of the world. People from all cultures believe in "constructive criticism." Yet what is considered constructive in one culture may be viewed as destructive in another. Getting negative feedback right can motivate your employees and strengthen your reputation as a fair and professional colleague. Getting it wrong can demoralize an entire team and earn you an undeserved reputation as an unfeeling tyrant or a hopelessly incompetent manager.

## SPEAKING FRANKLY: A GIFT OR A SLAP IN THE FACE?

One Thursday in mid-January, I had been holed up for six hours in a dark conference room with twelve people participating in my executive education program. It was a group coaching day, and each executive had thirty minutes to describe in detail a cross-cultural challenge she was experiencing at work and to get feedback and suggestions from the others at the table. The details of each person's situation were steeped in context, and I was beginning to get a headache from concentrating on the ins and outs of each challenge. We had made it through nine people and were just beginning with Willem, number ten.

Willem was a rather shy manager from the Netherlands, and, given his quiet persona, it struck me as unusual that he was a sales director. He had grey, slightly disheveled hair and a very friendly smile that made me think of a lovable St. Bernard. Willem's situation involved an American woman on his team who would call into team meetings while driving her children to school, a necessity given the six-hour time difference between her home in the eastern United States and Rotterdam. When Willem spoke to her about the distraction of screaming kids in the background and asked her to find a better solution, she took offense. "How can I fix this relationship?" Willem asked the group.

Maarten, the other Dutch member from the same company who knew Willem well, quickly jumped in with his perspective. "You are inflexible and can be socially ill-at-ease. That makes it difficult for you to communicate with your team," he reflected. As Willem listened, I could see his ears turning red (with embarrassment or anger? I wasn't sure), but that didn't seem to bother Maarten, who calmly continued to assess Willem's weaknesses in front of the entire group. Meanwhile, the other participants—all Americans—awkwardly stared at their feet. Afterward, several of them came up to me to say how inappropriate they'd found Maarten's comments.

For that evening, we'd planned a group dinner at a cozy restaurant in the French countryside. Entering a little after the others, I was startled to see Willem and Maarten sitting together, eating peanuts, drinking champagne, and laughing like old friends. They waved me over, and it seemed appropriate to comment, "I'm glad to see you together. I was afraid you might not be speaking to each other after the feedback session this afternoon." Willem stared at me in genuine surprise. So I clarified, "You looked upset when Maarten was giving his feedback. But maybe I misread the situation?"

Willem reflected, "Of course, I didn't *enjoy* hearing those things about myself. It doesn't feel good to hear what I have done poorly. But I so much appreciated that Maarten would be transparent enough to give me that feedback honestly. Feedback like that is a gift. Thanks for that, Maarten," he added with an appreciative smile.

I thought to myself, "This Dutch culture is . . . well . . . *different* from my own."

There has surely been a time when you were on the receiving end of criticism that was just too direct. You finished an important project and after asking a colleague for feedback, she told you it was "totally unprofessional." Or maybe a member of your team critiqued a grant proposal you wrote by calling it "ridiculously ineffective." You probably found this incident extremely painful; you may have felt this colleague was arrogant, and it's likely you rejected the advice offered. You may have developed a strong sense of distaste for this person that lingers to this day.

You may have also experienced the opposite—feedback that was far too indirect at a time when an honest assessment of your work would have been very valuable. Perhaps you asked a colleague for her thoughts about a project and were told, "Overall it's good. Some parts are great, and I particularly liked certain sections." Maybe she then noted that there were just a few very minor details that you might consider adjusting a bit, using phrases like "no big deal" and "just a very small thought," that left you thinking your work was nearly perfect.

If you later learned through the office grapevine that this same colleague had ridiculed your project behind your back as "the worst she'd seen in years," you probably were not very pleased. You likely felt a deep sense of betrayal leading to a lasting feeling of mistrust toward your colleague, now exposed in your eyes as a liar or a hypocrite.

Arrogance and dishonesty do exist, of course. There are even times when people give offense deliberately in pursuit of political objectives or in response to personal emotional problems. But in some cases, painful incidents like the ones just described are the result of cross-cultural misunderstandings. Managers in different parts of the world are conditioned to give feedback in drastically different ways. The Chinese manager learns never to criticize a colleague openly or in front of others, while the Dutch manager learns always to be honest and to give the message straight. Americans are trained to wrap positive messages around negative ones, while the French are trained to criticize passionately and provide positive feedback sparingly.

Having a clear understanding of these differences and strategies for navigating them is crucial for leaders of cross-cultural teams.

## UPGRADERS, DOWNGRADERS, AND THE ART OF TRANSLATION

One way to begin gauging how a culture handles negative feedback is by listening carefully to the types of words people use. More direct cultures tend to use what linguists call *upgraders*, words preceding or following negative feedback that make it feel stronger, such as *absolutely, totally,* or *strongly*: "This is *absolutely* inappropriate," or "This is *totally* unprofessional."

By contrast, more indirect cultures use more *downgraders*, words that soften the criticism, such as *kind of, sort of, a little, a bit, maybe,* and *slightly*. Another type of downgrader is a deliberate understatement, a sentence that describes a feeling the speaker experiences strongly in terms that moderate the emotion—for example, saying "We are not quite there yet" when you really mean "This is nowhere close to complete," or "This is just my opinion" when you really mean "Anyone who considers this issue will immediately agree."

For many years I worked with Amihan Castillo, a lawyer and business professor from the Philippines who'd come to work in Europe following a highly successful career in Manila. Unfortunately, her opinions went unnoticed when working with our European team because she was so careful to downgrade any criticisms she made of proposals and projects. For example, if we were preparing a descriptive brochure for a new executive program, Castillo might comment on the cover design by saying, "Hmm, I thought we might possibly consider giving a bolder look to the brochure cover . . . maybe? What do you think?" A European or an American would probably convey the same feeling by saying, "The look of the cover isn't working. I suggest we try this." Only after years of working with Castillo had I learned to interpret her messages correctly.

Of course, downgraders are used in every world culture, but some cultures use them more than others. The British are masters of the art, with the result that their communications often leave the rest of us quite bewildered. Take the announcement made by British Airways pilot Eric Moody in 1982, after flying through a cloud of volcanic ash over Indonesia: "Good evening again, ladies and gentlemen. This is Captain Eric Moody here. We have a small problem in that all four engines have failed. We're doing our utmost to get them going and I trust you're not in too much distress, and would the chief steward please come to the flight deck?"

Fortunately, the plane was able to glide far enough to exit the ash cloud and the engines were restarted, allowing the aircraft to land safely at the Halim Perdanakusuma Airport in Jakarta with no casualties. Moody's recorded announcement has since been widely hailed as a classic example of understatement.

The "Anglo-Dutch Translation Guide" (Figure 2.1), which has been anonymously circulating in various versions on the Internet, amusingly illustrates how the British use downgraders and the resulting confusion this can create among listeners from another culture (in this case, the Dutch).[1]

For Marcus Klopfer, a German finance director at the management consulting firm KPMG, such cross-cultural misunderstandings

### FIGURE 2.1. ANGLO-DUTCH TRANSLATION GUIDE

| What the British say | What the British mean | What the Dutch understand |
| --- | --- | --- |
| With all due respect... | I think you are wrong. | He is listening to me. |
| Perhaps you would think about...I would suggest... | This is an order. Do it or be prepared to justify yourself. | Think about this idea and do it if you like. |
| Oh, by the way... | The following criticism is the purpose of this discussion. | This is not very important. |
| I was a bit disappointed that... | I am very upset and angry that... | It doesn't really matter. |
| Very interesting... | I don't like it. | He is impressed. |
| Could you consider some other options? | Your idea is not a good one. | He has not yet decided. |
| Please think about that some more. | It's a bad idea. Don't do it. | It's a good idea. Keep developing it. |
| I'm sure it's my fault. | It's not my fault. | It's his fault. |
| That is an original point of view. | Your idea is stupid. | He likes my idea! |

Source: Nanette Ripmeester

are no laughing matter. A soft-spoken manager in his forties, Klopfer described how his failure to decode a message from his British boss almost cost him his job:

> In Germany, we typically use strong words when complaining or criticizing in order to make sure the message registers clearly and honestly. Of course, we assume others will do the same. My British boss during a one-on-one "suggested that I think about" doing something differently. So I took his suggestion: I thought about it and decided not to do it. Little did I know that his phrase was supposed to be interpreted as "change your behavior right away or else." And I can tell you I was pretty surprised when my boss called me into his office to chew me out for insubordination!
>
> I learned then and there that I needed to ignore all of the soft words surrounding the message when listening to my British teammates and just analyze the message as if it were given to me raw. Of course, the other lesson was to consider how my British staff might interpret my messages, which I had been delivering as "purely" as possible with no softeners whatsoever. I realize now that when I give feedback in my German way, I may actually use words that make the message sound as strong as possible without thinking much about it. I've been surrounded by this "pure" negative feedback since I was a child.

Now Klopfer makes a concerted effort to soften the message when giving negative feedback to his British counterparts:

> I try to start by sprinkling the ground with a few light positive comments and words of appreciation. Then I ease into the feedback with "a few small suggestions." As I'm giving the feedback, I add words like "minor" or "possibly." Then I wrap up by

stating that "This is just my opinion, for whatever it is worth," and "You can take it or leave it."

The elaborate dance is quite humorous from a German's point of view. We'd be much more comfortable just stating *Das war absolut unverschämt* ("that was absolutely shameless"). But it certainly gets my desired results!

The Evaluating scale (Figure 2.2) provides a bird's-eye view of just how direct people in different cultures are with negative criticism. You can see that most European countries fall to the direct side of the scale, with the Russians, Dutch, and Germans as particularly prone to offering frank criticism.

American culture is in the middle of the scale; nearby are the British, who are slightly less direct with negative feedback than Americans. Latin Americans and South Americans fall to the middle right, with Argentina as one of the most direct of this

### FIGURE 2.2. **EVALUATING**

| Russia | France | | Italy | US | UK | Brazil | India | Saudi Arabia | Japan |
| Israel | Germany | Norway | Australia | | Canada | Mexico | China | Korea | Thailand |
| Netherlands | Denmark | | Spain | | | Argentina | Kenya | Ghana | Indonesia |

⟵——————————————————————————————⟶

**Direct negative feedback**                     **Indirect negative feedback**

| **Direct negative feedback** | Negative feedback to a colleague is provided frankly, bluntly, honestly. Negative messages stand alone, not softened by positive ones. Absolute descriptors are often used (totally inappropriate, completely unprofessional) when criticizing. Criticism may be given to an individual in front of a group. |
|---|---|
| **Indirect negative feedback** | Negative feedback to a colleague is provided softly, subtly, diplomatically. Positive messages are used to wrap negative ones. Qualifying descriptors are often used (sort of inappropriate, slightly unprofessional) when criticizing. Criticism is given only in private. |

cluster. Further right on the scale fall most Asian countries, with the Indians as the most direct with their criticism and the Thai, Cambodians, Indonesians, and Japanese as the least direct.

Don't forget cultural relativity when you look at the scale. For example, the Chinese are to the right of the world scale, but they are much more direct than the Japanese, who may take offense at their forthright feedback. The continental European cultures to the left or middle often experience Americans as strikingly indirect, while Latin Americans perceive the same Americans as blunt and brutally frank in their criticism style.

Note, too, that several countries have different positions on the Evaluating scale from those they occupy on the Communicating scale. For this reason, you may be surprised by the gap between our stereotyped assumptions about certain countries and their placement on the Evaluating scale. The explanation lies in the fact that stereotypes about how directly people speak generally reflect their cultures' position on the Communicating scale, not the Evaluating scale. Thus, the French, Spanish, and Russians are generally stereotyped as being indirect communicators because of their high-context, implicit communication style, despite the fact that they give negative feedback more directly. Americans are stereotyped as direct by most of the world, yet when they give negative feedback they are less direct than many European cultures.

One high-context country on the direct side of the Evaluating scale is Israel, where people may speak with copious subtext, yet give some of the most direct negative feedback in the world. Once I was running a class for the World Medical Association that included a large number of Israeli doctors and a group of doctors from Singapore. One of the Singaporean doctors, a small woman in her fifties, protested vociferously when she saw the far left-hand positioning of Israel on the Evaluating scale. "I don't see how Israel can be positioned as so direct! We have been with our Israeli friends here all week and they are good, kind people!" From her Singaporean perspective being good was correlated with being diplomatic and being very direct was correlated with not being kind.

In response, one of the Israeli doctors declared, "I don't see what that has to do with it. Honesty and directness are a great virtues. The position is correct, and I am very proud of it." Israel is one of several cultures that value both high-context communication and direct negative feedback.

Mapping the Communicating scale against the Evaluating scale gives us four quadrants, as shown in Figure 2.3: low-context and direct with negative feedback; low-context and indirect with negative feedback; high-context and direct with negative feedback; and high-context and indirect with negative feedback. Particular cultures can be found in each of these quadrants, and there are differing strategies you'll find effective for dealing with people from each.

## LOW-CONTEXT AND DIRECT NEGATIVE FEEDBACK

Whether they're considered blunt, rude, and offensive or honest, transparent, and frank, these cultures are perceived as direct by all other world populations. Cultures in this quadrant (the quadrant labeled A in Figure 2.3) value low-context, explicit communication as well as direct negative feedback. The natural coherence of these two positions makes communication from people in this quadrant fairly easy to decode. Take any messages they send literally and understand that it is not intended to be offensive but rather as a simple sign of honesty, transparency, and respect for your own professionalism.

We already met Willem and Maarten who come from the Netherlands, a solidly quadrant A culture. Willem experienced

**FIGURE 2.3.**

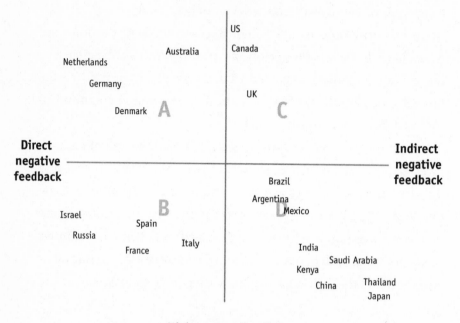

**Low-context/explicit**

US
Canada
Australia
Netherlands
Germany
UK
Denmark A
C

**Direct negative feedback** ────────────────── **Indirect negative feedback**

Brazil
Argentina
B
Israel Mexico
Spain
Russia
Italy
France
India
Saudi Arabia
Kenya
China Thailand
Japan

**High-context/implicit**

Maarten's explicit and direct negative feedback to be not just appropriate, but a real gift. What if Willem and Maarten were your colleagues? What is an appropriate way to respond to their direct style of offering criticism?

One rule for working with cultures that are more direct than yours on the Evaluating scale: *Don't try to do it like them.* Even in the countries farthest to the direct side of the Evaluating scale, it is still quite possible to be *too* direct. If you don't understand the subtle rules that separate what's appropriately frank from what is callously insensitive in Dutch culture, then leave it to someone from that culture to speak directly. If you try to do it like them, you run the risk of getting it wrong, going too far, and making unintended enemies.

I witnessed this type of mistake when working with a Korean manager named Kwang Young-Su who had been living in the Netherlands for six years. A friendly, quiet man in his early forties, Kwang had a wide grin and soft laugh that we heard frequently. But Kwang's colleagues had complained to me that they found him so aggressive and angry that they were practically unable to work with him. I wondered how this could be so, until Kwang himself explained the situation:

> The Dutch culture is very direct, and we Koreans do not like to give direct negative feedback. So when I first came to the Netherlands, I was shocked at how rude and arrogant the Dutch are with their criticism. When they don't like something, they tell you bluntly to your face. I spoke to another Korean friend who has been in the Netherlands for a while, and he told me that the only way to handle this is to give it right back to them. Now I try to be just as blunt with them as they are with me.

Unfortunately, not understanding the subtleties of what was appropriate and what was not, Kwang had gone too far, missing the mark entirely. He alienated his colleagues, sabotaged his relationships, and built up a reputation as an angry aggressor. So much for adaptability.

Don't make the same mistake as Kwang. When you are working with cultures from quadrant A, accept their direct criticism in a positive manner. It is not meant to offend you. But don't take the risk of trying to do it like them. One small upgrader at a time may be all you can risk without tipping over to the side of being offensive or inappropriate.

## HIGH-CONTEXT AND DIRECT NEGATIVE FEEDBACK

Quadrant B (see page 72) is populated with those puzzlingly complex cultures that have finessed the ability to speak and listen between the lines yet give negative feedback that is sharp and direct. Russians, for example, often pass messages between the lines, but when it comes to criticism they have a directness that can startle their international colleagues.

The first time I traveled to Russia a Russian friend gave me a short little book that she referred to as "The Russian Handbook."[2] Paging through the book during my flight, I was amused to read:

> If you are walking through the street without a jacket, little old Russian ladies may stop and chastise you for poor judgment. . . . In Russia there is no reticence about expressing your negative criticism openly. For instance, if you are displeased with the service in a shop or restaurant you can tell the shop assistant or waiter exactly what you think of him, his relatives, his in-laws, his habits, and his sexual bias.

I thought about this observation a few weeks later when I received a call from a British colleague, Sandi Carlson. She explained to me that a young Russian woman named Anna Golov had recently joined her team and was upsetting a lot of people whose help she needed to get her job done. "I'm calling you, Erin," she said, "because I wondered if the problem might be cultural. This is the fourth Russian coordinator we have had in the group, and with three of them there were similar types of complaints about harsh criticism or what has been perceived as speaking to others inconsiderately."

A few days later, I had the opportunity to witness the problem in action. While I prepared to teach one morning, Golov herself was in the room with me setting up the classroom. I was going through stacks of handouts, counting pages to make sure we had enough photocopies, while Golov was carefully checking the IT equipment, which, to our annoyance, was not working properly. I appreciated the fact that she was handling the problem with such tenacity and that I did not have to get involved. The fact that she was humming quietly while she worked gave me an extra sense of relaxed assurance.

But then I heard Golov on the phone with someone in the IT department. "I've called IT three times this week, and every time you are slow to get here and the solution doesn't last," she complained. "The solutions you have given me are entirely unacceptable." Golov went on scolding the IT manager, each sentence a bit harsher than the one before. I held my breath. Was she going to tell him how she felt about his sexual bias? Thankfully not at that moment.

Later, Carlson asked me, as the resident cross-cultural specialist, whether I would accompany her when she spoke with Golov about the problem. I was not thrilled at the request. I certainly did not look forward to witnessing Golov learn what her new colleagues were saying about her behind her back. But at Carlson's insistence, I agreed.

We met in Carlson's office, and she tried to explain the reputation that Golov had unknowingly developed across the campus, citing specific complaints not just from the IT department but also from the photocopying staff. Golov shifted uncomfortably in her chair while Carlson explained that she had wondered whether the problem was cultural.

At first Anna did not really understand the feedback. She protested, "But we Russians are very subtle communicators.

We use irony and subtext. You British and Americans speak so transparently."

"Yes," I interjected. "But if a Russian has negative feedback to give, it seems that often that feedback is perceived to be harsh or direct to people from other cultures. Does that make sense?"

"Yes, well . . . that depends who we are speaking with, of course. One point is that we tend to be a very hierarchical culture. If you are a boss speaking to your subordinate, you may be very frank. And if you are a subordinate speaking to your boss, you had better be very diplomatic with criticism." Carlson smiled, perhaps realizing why she had never personally experienced any of Golov's frankness.

Golov went on:

If we are speaking with strangers, we often speak very forcefully. This is true. These IT guys, I don't know them. They are the voices of strangers on the other end of the phone. Under Communism, the stranger was the enemy. We didn't know who we could trust, who would turn us in to the authorities, who would betray us. So we kept strangers at a forceful distance. Maybe I brought a little too much of my Russian-ness into the job without realizing it.

I noticed that Golov was now beginning to laugh a little as she continued to consider the situation. "We are also very direct with people we are close to," she conceded reflectively. "My British friends here complain that I voice my opinions so strongly, while I feel like I never know how they really feel about the situation. I am always saying: 'But how do you feel about it?' And they are always responding: 'Why are you always judging everything?'!"

"Now that I'm aware of this," Golov concluded, "I'll be more careful when I communicate dissatisfaction."

The French have a saying, *"Quand on connait sa maladie, on est à moitié guéri"*—"When you know your sickness, you are halfway cured." It applies to most cross-cultural confusions. Just building your own awareness and the awareness of your team goes a long way to improving collaboration. Now that Carlson is aware of the cultural tendencies impacting the situation, she can talk to Golov and her team about it, and Golov can take steps to give less direct criticism and replace some of her upgraders with downgraders. When it comes to the Evaluating scale, a few simple words can make all the difference.

## LOW-CONTEXT AND INDIRECT NEGATIVE FEEDBACK

Combining extreme low-context communication with a mid-indirect approach to giving negative feedback, the American evaluating style (quadrant C in Figure 2.3, page 72) is so specific, unique, and often baffling to the rest of the world that it deserves a few paragraphs to itself.

An explicit, low-context communication style gives Americans the reputation of lacking subtlety. Leave it to the Americans to point out the elephant in the room when the rest of us were working through our interpersonal issues nicely without calling attention to it. This means that those in quadrants A and B are often surprised to find Americans softening negative criticism with positive messages. Before moving to France, having been raised, educated, and employed in the United States, I believed that giving three positives for every negative and beginning a feedback session with the words of explicit appreciation before discussing what needs to be improved were universally effective techniques. If they worked well in America, then surely they should work just as well in France, Brazil, China and, well, everywhere.

But after living in Europe for a while I learned to see this style from a completely different perspective. To the French, Spanish, Russians, Dutch, and Germans, the American mode of giving feedback comes across as false and confusing. Willem, who we met at the beginning of the chapter and who works frequently with Americans, told me:

> To a Dutchman, it is all a lot of hogwash. All that positive feedback just strikes us as fake and not in the least bit motivating. I was on a conference call with an American group yesterday, and the organizer began, "I am absolutely thrilled to be with you this morning." *Only* an American would begin a meeting like this. Let's face it, everyone in the room knows that she is not truly, honestly thrilled. Thrilled to win the lottery—yes. Thrilled to find out that you have won a free trip to the Caribbean—yes. Thrilled to be the leader of a conference call— highly doubtful.
>
> When my American colleagues begin a communication with all of their "excellents" and "greats," it feels so exaggerated that I find it demeaning. We are adults, here to do our jobs and to do them well. We don't need our colleagues to be cheerleaders.

Willem's colleague Maarten added:

> The problem is that we can't tell when the feedback is supposed to register to us as excellent, okay, or really poor. For a Dutchman, the word "excellent" is saved for a rare occasion

and "okay" is . . . well, neutral. But with the Americans, the grid is different. "Excellent" is used all the time. "Okay" seems to mean "not okay." "Good" is only a mild compliment. And when the message was intended to be bad, you can pretty much assume that, if an American is speaking and the listener is Dutch, the real meaning of the message will be lost all together.

The same difference is reflected in the ways children are treated in schools. My children are in the French school system during the academic year and spend the summer in American academic programs in the Minneapolis area. In the United States, my eight-year-old son, Ethan, gets his homework assignments back covered with gold stars and comments like "Keep it up!" "Excellent work!" and, at worst, "Almost there . . . give it another try!" But studying in Madame Durand's class requires thicker skin. After a recent Monday morning spelling test, Ethan's notebook page was covered sorrowfully in red lines and fat Xs, along with seven simple words from Madame Durand: "8 errors. Skills not acquired. Apply yourself!"

Ooooof! That hurts a mom from Minnesota. What about "Nice effort!" or "Don't give up!" or "You'll get it next time"? And I should note that Madame Durand is known as the least "sévère," that is, the softest of the teachers at Ethan's school.

At first, I worried that Ethan might begin to hate school, dislike his teacher, become discouraged, or just plain stop trying. But to the surprise of his American mom, he is coming to interpret negative feedback as the French would. The scathing comments strike him as routine, while a rare "TB" (*très bien*—very good) leaves a deeply positive impression on his young psyche.

However, adapting to quadrant C can be quite challenging for those from other cultures. Frenchwoman Sabine Dulac recalls an experience that happened soon after her move to Chicago:

> Along with a group of American colleagues, I was on a committee which was organizing a big conference to market our new product line to current clients. The conference was a disaster. There was a horrible icy rainstorm that morning, which meant low attendance. The keynote speaker was a bore. The food was horrible.
>
> Afterward the committee met to debrief the conference. Everyone knew the conference had been a disastrous failure, but when the team leader asked for feedback, each committee member started by mentioning something good about the conference: the booths had been well organized, the buses to the restaurant were on time, . . . before moving on to the calamities. I was stunned. I actually had to hold my jaw closed while I watched my colleagues detailing positive example after positive example in describing a situation that was so clearly anything but.
>
> When it was my turn, I couldn't take it anymore—I just launched right in. "It was one disappointment after another," I began. "The keynote was uninspiring, the food was almost inedible, the breakout sessions were boring . . . ," but as I spoke I saw the Americans around me staring at me saucer-eyed and silent. Did I have food on my face, I wondered?

People in Dulac's position can follow a few simple strategies to work more effectively with people from quadrant C (that is, Americans, British, and Canadians).

First, when providing an evaluation, *be explicit and low-context with both positive and negative feedback.* But don't launch into the negatives until you have also explicitly stated something that you appreciate about the person or the situation. The positive comments should be honest and stated in a detailed, explicit manner.

When I gave Dulac this suggestion, her first reaction was to feel that I was asking her to lie. "If I thought the conference was a total disaster, isn't it dishonest to not say what I think?"

But I pressed her: Wasn't there anything honest and positive that she could say about the conference? Dulac considered the question and came up with a couple of ideas. After I explained the differing attitudes of Americans toward the "proper" way of delivering feedback, Dulac understood the kind of adjustment she needed to make:

> If I were in that situation again, I might start by talking about how much we learned from the event about what to do differently next time. I might also mention how impressed I was that there were no IT snafus, thanks to the logistical staff led by the always tenacious and hardworking Marion. And then, when I get to the disaster part, I might use a downgrader. "It was a bit of a disaster" might go over better than "a total disaster" the next time around.

Second, *try, over time, to be balanced in the amount of positive and negative feedback you give.* For example, if you notice something positive your colleague has done on Monday, say it there and then with explicit, open appreciation. Then, on Tuesday, when you need to severely criticize the same colleague's disappointing proposal before it is sent to the client, your comments will be more likely to be heard and considered rather than rejected out of hand.

Third, *frame your behavior in cultural terms.* Talk about the cultural differences that explain your communication style. If possible, show appreciation for the other culture while laughing humbly at your own. Someone in Dulac's position might say, "In the U.S., you are so good at openly appreciating one another. In France, we aren't in the habit of voicing positive feedback. We might think it, but we don't say it!"

To those she works with frequently, Dulac might also explain her natural feedback style: "When I say 'okay,' you should hear 'very good.' And when I say 'good,' you should hear 'excellent.'"

Framing comments like these builds awareness among people on both sides of the table and may lead to useful discussions about other cultural misunderstandings.

## HIGH-CONTEXT AND INDIRECT NEGATIVE FEEDBACK

Among people from cultures in quadrant D as shown on page 72, negative feedback is generally soft, subtle, and implicit. Turn your head too quickly and you might miss the negative message altogether. Whereas in American culture you might give negative feedback in public by veiling it in a joking or friendly manner, in quadrant D this would be unacceptable; any negative feedback should be given in private, regardless of how much humor or good-natured ribbing you wrap around it.

Charlie Hammer, an American manager in the textile industry living and working in Mexico City, offers this example:

> I was really taken aback when one of my Mexican employees gave me his resignation. I had given him some negative feedback in a meeting, but I did it in a way that sounded to me almost like a joke. The mood in the room was light, and after giving the feedback I quickly moved on. I felt it was no big deal and I thought everything was fine. But apparently it was a big deal to him. I learned later from one of the team members that I had seriously insulted him by giving this feedback in front of the team. He felt

humiliated and worried that he was going to get fired, so he decided it would be better to quit first. It took me completely by surprise.

As this situation suggests, the first simple strategy for giving negative feedback to someone from a culture in quadrant D is *Don't give feedback to an individual in front of a group.* This rule applies even if you use a lot of soft, cozy downgraders or rely on a joke to lighten the mood. And, yes, it applies to positive feedback as well. In many cultures that are less individualistic than the United States, it may be embarrassing to be singled out for positive praise in front of others. Give your individual feedback to the individual and give only group feedback to the group.

A second powerful tool for giving feedback to those from quadrant D—especially those from Asian cultures—is the technique of *blurring the message.* People from most Western cultures don't like the idea of making a message blurry. We like our messages short, crisp, and, above all, transparent. But blurriness can be highly effective in many Asian cultures if it is used skillfully and appropriately, as I discovered early in my career.

I had been working as a consultant for an international training firm for about a year. One of my programs was a custom-designed international leadership course for the large Swiss-headquartered food multinational Nestlé. I co-taught the program with Budi, an Indonesian consultant who had been with the company for decades and was close to the founders. He had a reputation as a highly skilled trainer, but over the last couple of years his classroom performance had been declining dramatically, much to everyone's chagrin.

Let me also add that it was politically useful to have Budi on your side. As someone very well connected within the organization, he could open many doors if he liked you, and he had done so for many of his favored colleagues in the past.

With all of this in mind, I winced when my contact at Nestlé gave me quite clear feedback that they wanted to eliminate two of the three sessions that Budi taught in the program based on mediocre evaluation ratings.

I went home that evening with a knot in my stomach. When Budi heard that I was replacing his sessions with two sessions led by a more junior consultant, he was likely to be hurt and embarrassed. To complicate an already difficult situation, Budi comes from one of the most indirect cultures in the world, where giving negative feedback to someone older and more experienced is particularly difficult and painful. I didn't sleep well that night.

The next morning in an anxious stupor I set up a lunch with a longtime Indonesian colleague and friend and asked her for advice. Thankfully, Aini introduced me to some strategies for blurring the message.

The first strategy: *Give the feedback slowly, over a period of time, so that it gradually sinks in.* "In the West," Aini said, "you learn that feedback should be given right here, right now. In most Asian societies, it is best to give feedback gradually. This does not mean that you beat the direct message in periodically, again and again. Rather it means that you make small references to the changes that need to be made gently, gradually building a clear picture as to what should be done differently."

With Aini's guidance, I composed a first e-mail to Budi, alluding to the fact that I would need to redesign the program in future months based on the feedback of the participants and that this would have an impact on his sessions. I mentioned that I needed to focus more on topic X, which meant we would have less time for topic Y. Budi responded kindly, saying that he would be pleased to discuss it with me when he was in Paris later that month.

Budi and I spoke by phone the week before his visit to Paris, and I mentioned that I would be sending the most recent client feedback so that he could see it before our meeting. I indicated that the program would be reworked entirely and that I would also be inviting our junior colleague to teach in some sessions. Bit by bit, Budi was beginning to get the picture.

This led to Aini's second strategy: *Use food and drink to blur an unpleasant message.* Aini told me, "If I have to provide criticism to someone on my staff, I am not going to call them into my office. If I do, I know that they are going to be listening to my message with all of their senses—and any message I provide will be greatly amplified in their minds. Instead, I might invite them out to lunch. Once we are relaxed, this is a good time to give feedback. We don't make reference to it in the office the next day or the next week, but the feedback has been passed and the receiver is now able to take action without humiliation or breaking the harmony between the two parties. In Japan, Thailand, Korea, China, or Indonesia, the same strategy applies."

This would be an easy rule to apply. I told Budi that when he was in Paris I would love to have lunch with him at my favorite new restaurant near the Champs-Elysées, where I knew he would love the black squid pasta.

Aini's third and final piece of strategy baffled me at first. She urged me: *Say the good and leave out the bad.* Was Aini suggesting that I could pass the negative message without saying it at all? Via telepathy?

Aini explained by using an example:

A while back, one of my Indonesian colleagues sent me a set of four documents to read and review. The last two documents he must have finished in a hurry, because they were very sloppy in comparison to the first two. When he called to ask for my reaction, I told him that the first two papers were excellent. I focused on these documents only, outlining *why* they were so effective. I didn't need to mention the sloppy documents, which would have been uncomfortable for both of us. He got the message clearly, and I didn't even need to bring up the negative aspects.

Well, I understood the concept, although the execution for someone from Two Harbors, Minnesota, was not easy.

The next week, I met Budi at the Italian bistro I had told him about. After forty-five minutes of catching up over delicious artichoke hearts and sun-dried tomato antipasti, the moment of truth had come. "Say the good, leave out the bad," I reminded myself, easing gently into the subject, my heart beating just a little faster than normal.

"Budi," I began, "your first session is very much appreciated. Although I am redesigning the program, I definitely do not want to touch this session. In fact, I thought I might build on your first session by working with our junior colleague on Tuesday morning's session."

Budi replied, "That sounds great, Erin! I much prefer to have a shorter amount of presentation time with a really big impact. And if that works for the program, it works for me."

Hallelujah! Not a moment of discomfort! I had somehow managed to pass the message without ever giving the criticism explicitly. Thank you, Aini!

Here is one final warning for anyone working with people from a quadrant D culture. While indirect feedback is the norm, it is quite possible for a boss to give scathing negative feedback to an employee while remaining entirely within the realm of the appropriate. In these cases, the strongly hierarchical tendencies found in many quadrant D cultures trump their indirect feedback patterns. Thus, it's not unheard of for a boss in Korea to berate an employee publicly or for an Indian boss to bark criticism to their staff in a way that shocks and silences any Europeans or Americans within earshot.

But you, the foreigner, should not try this. For your purposes, whether you are the mail boy, the manager, or the owner of the company, stick to the blurring and leave the direct downward vertical feedback to those who call that country home.

## WHAT DOES IT MEAN TO BE POLITE?

Maarten, the Dutch manager we met earlier, explained to me once, "In the Netherlands, we give feedback very directly, but we are always polite." I love this comment, because a Dutch person's feedback can indeed be both brutally honest yet delightfully polite—but only if the recipient is Dutch. If you happen to come from one of the 195 or so societies in the world that like their negative feedback a bit less direct than in the Netherlands, you may feel that Maarten's "politeness" is downright insulting, offensive, and yes, rude.

Politeness is in the eye of the beholder. Giving feedback—especially when it's negative—is a sensitive business at the best of times. It can be made a lot worse if the person receiving the feedback believes he or she has been spoken to rudely. Precisely what constitutes rudeness, however, varies enormously from place to place.

The sophisticated global manager learns how to adapt—to alter his behavior a bit, to practice humility, to test the waters before speaking up, to assume goodwill on the part of others, and to invest time and energy in building good relationships. With a little luck and skill, it's possible to be perceived as equally polite in Amsterdam, Jakarta, Moscow, Buenos Aires, Paris, or Two Harbors, Minnesota.

# 3

## Why Versus How

The Art of Persuasion
in a Multicultural World

The art of persuasion is one of the most crucial business skills. Without the ability to persuade others to support your ideas, you won't be able to attract the support you need to turn those ideas into realities. And though most people are unaware of it, the ways you seek to persuade others and the kinds of arguments you find persuasive are deeply rooted in your culture's philosophical, religious, and educational assumptions and attitudes. Far from being universal, then, the art of persuasion is one that is profoundly culture-based.

That was the hard lesson learned by Kara Williams, an American engineer newly working as a research manager for a German firm in the automotive industry. As one of the leading experts in her field Williams had extensive experience presenting recommendations and influencing her American colleagues to follow her ideas. But when Williams began working in a German environment she didn't realize that being persuasive would require a different approach. "When I think back to my first presentation to my new German bosses, I wish I had understood the difference and hadn't let their feedback get under my skin. If I had held my cool I might have been able to salvage the situation."

Williams has faced many challenges in her career. Before taking the job with the German firm, she worked for an Australian company from her home office in Boston, traveling frequently to the Sydney headquarters to give presentations and offer advice. "A lot of my job relies on my ability to sell my ideas and influence my internal clients to take the best path," she explains. "I'm good at what I do, but I hate constant long-distance travel. When offered a similar position working for a German auto supplier, I jumped at the opportunity for shorter travel distances."

Williams's first project was providing technical advice on how to reduce carbon emissions from one of the group's "green" car models. After visiting several automotive plants, observing the systems and processes there, and meeting with dozens of experts and end users, Williams developed a set of recommendations that she felt would meet the company's strategic and budgetary goals. She traveled to Munich to give a one-hour presentation to the decision makers—a group of German directors.

"It was my first internal presentation, and its success would be important for my reputation," Williams recalls. In preparation for the meeting Williams thought carefully about how to give the most persuasive presentation, practicing her arguments, anticipating questions that might arise, and preparing responses to those questions.

Williams delivered her presentation in a small auditorium with the directors seated in rows of upholstered chairs. She began by getting right to the point, explaining the strategies she would recommend based on her findings. But before she had finished with the first slide, one of the directors raised his hand and protested, "How did you get to these conclusions? You are giving us your recommendations, but I don't understand how you got here. How many people did you interview? What questions did you ask?"

Then another director jumped in: "Please explain what methodology you used for analyzing your data and how that led you to come to these findings."

"I was taken aback," Williams remembers. "I assured them that the methodology behind my recommendations was sound, but the questions and challenges continued. The more they questioned me, the more I got the feeling that they were attacking my credibility, which puzzled and annoyed me. I have a Ph.D. in engineering and expertise that is widely acknowledged. Their effort to test my conclusions, I felt, showed a real lack of respect. What arrogance to think that they would be better able to judge than I am!"

Williams reacted defensively, and the presentation went downhill from there. "I kick myself now for having allowed their approach to derail my point," she says. "Needless to say, they did not approve my recommendations, and three months of research time went down the drain."

The stone wall Williams ran into illustrates the hard truth that our ability to persuade others depends not simply on the strength of our message but on how we build our arguments and the persuasive techniques we employ.

Jens Hupert is a German director at the company Williams worked for. Having lived in the United States for many years, he had experienced similar failures at persuading others, though the cultural disconnect ran in the opposite direction. Hupert recalled the problems he'd had the first few times he tried to make a persuasive argument before a group of his American colleagues. He'd carefully launched his presentation by laying the foundation for his conclusions, setting the parameters, outlining his data and his methodology, and explaining the premise of his argument. He was taken aback when his American boss told him, "In your next pre-sentation, get right to the point. You lost their attention before you even got to the important part."

Hupert was unsure. "These are intelligent people," he thought. "Why would they swallow my argument if I haven't built it care-fully for them from the ground up?"

The opposing reactions that Williams and Hupert received re-flect the cultural differences between German and American styles of persuasion. The approach taken by the Germans is based on a specific style of reasoning that is deeply ingrained in the cultural psyche. Hupert explains:

> In Germany, we try to understand the theoretical concept before adapting it to the practical situation. To understand something, we first want to analyze all of the conceptual data before coming to a conclusion. When colleagues from cul-tures like the U.S. or the U.K. make presentations to us, we don't realize that they were taught to think differently from us. So when they begin by presenting conclusions and rec-ommendations without setting up the parameters and how they got to those conclusions, it can actually shock us. We may feel insulted. Do they think we are stupid—that we will just swallow anything? Or we may question whether their deci-sion was well thought out. This reaction is based on our deep-seated belief that you cannot come to a conclusion without first defining the parameters.

Hupert's time in the United States taught him that Americans have a very different approach. They focus on practicalities rather than theory, so they are much more likely to begin with their rec-ommendations. Unfortunately, this reasoning method can backfire when making presentations to an audience whose method of thinking is the opposite—as Kara Williams discovered.

## TWO STYLES OF REASONING: PRINCIPLES-FIRST VERSUS APPLICATIONS-FIRST

*Principles-first reasoning* (sometimes referred to as *deductive reasoning*) derives conclusions or facts from general principles or concepts. For example, we may start with a general principle like "All men are mortal." Then we move to a more specific example: "Justin Bieber is a man." This leads us to the conclusion, "Justin Bieber will, eventually, die." Similarly, we may start with the general principle "Everything made of copper conducts electricity." Then we show that the old statue of a leprechaun your grandmother left you is 100 percent copper. Based on these points, we can arrive at the conclusion, "Your grandmother's statue will conduct electricity." In both examples, we started with the general principle and moved from it to a practical conclusion.

On the other hand, with *applications-first reasoning* (sometimes called *inductive reasoning*), general conclusions are reached based on a pattern of factual observations from the real world. For example, if you travel to my hometown in Minnesota one hundred times during January and February, and you observe every visit that the temperature is considerably below zero, you will conclude that Minnesota winters are cold (and that a winter visit to Minnesota calls for a warm coat as well as a scarf, wool hat, gloves, and ear warmers). In this case, you observe data from the real world, and, based on these empirical observations, you draw broader conclusions.

Most people are capable of practicing both principles-first and applications-first reasoning. But your habitual pattern of reasoning is heavily influenced by the kind of thinking emphasized in your culture's educational structure. As a result, you can quickly run into problems when working with people who are most accustomed to other modes of reasoning.

Take math class as an example. In a course using the applications-first method, you first learn the formula and practice applying it. After seeing how this formula leads to the right answer again and again, you then move on to understand the concept or principle underpinning it. This means you may spend 80 percent of your time focusing on the concrete tool and how to apply it and only 20 percent of your time considering its conceptual or theoretical explanation. School systems in Anglo-Saxon countries tend to emphasize this method of teaching.

By contrast, in a principles-first math class, you first prove the general principle, and only then use it to develop a concrete formula that can be applied to various problems. As a French manager once told me, "We had to calculate the value of pi as a class before we used pi in a formula." In this kind of math class, you may spend 80 percent of your time focusing on the concepts or theories underpinning the general mathematical principles and only 20 percent of your time applying those principles to concrete problems. School systems in Latin Europe (France, Italy, Spain, Portugal), the Germanic countries (Germany, Austria), and Latin America (Mexico, Brazil, Argentina) tend to emphasize this method of teaching.

I felt the full force of the applications-first method when I studied Russian in my American high school. We walked into Mr. Tarasov's class on the first day of school, and he immediately fired questions at us in Russian. We didn't understand a thing. But gradually we started to understand, and, after a few lessons, we began to speak, putting words together any which way we could. Then, with Mr. Tarasov's guidance, we began using sentences whose structure we did not understand to create a conceptual grammatical framework.

By contrast, in a principles-first language class, learning starts with understanding the grammatical principles underpinning the language structure. Once you have a solid initial grasp of the grammar and vocabulary, you begin to practice using the language. This is the way my husband learned English in his French school, and ironically, his knowledge of English grammar is far superior to that of many Americans. The disadvantage is that students spend less time practicing the language, which may mean they write it better than they speak it.

In business, as in school, people from principles-first cultures generally want to understand the *why* behind their boss's request before they move to action. Meanwhile, applications-first learners tend to focus less on the *why* and more on the *how*. One of the most common frustrations among French employees with American bosses is that the American tells them what to do without explaining why they need to do it. From the French perspective, this can feel demotivating, even disrespectful. By contrast, American bosses may feel that French workers are uncooperative because, instead of acting quickly, they always ask "Why?" and are not ready to act until they have received a suitable response.

## COUNTRY POSITIONS ON THE PERSUADING SCALE

In general, Anglo-Saxon cultures like the United States, the United Kingdom, Australia, Canada, and New Zealand tend to fall to the far right on the Persuading scale (see Figure 3.1), where applications-first cultures are clustered. As we move across the scale there's a Nordic cluster, where we find Scandinavia and the

## FIGURE 3.1. **PERSUADING**

| Italy | Russia | Germany | Argentina | Sweden | Netherlands | Australia | |
| France | Spain | | Brazil | Mexico | Denmark | UK | Canada | US |

←————————————————————————————————————————————→

**Principles-first**                                                    **Applications-first**

......................................................................................................

**Principles-first**  Individuals are trained to begin with a fact, statement, or opinion and later add concepts to back up or explain the conclusion as necessary. The preference is to begin a message or report with an executive summary or bullet points. Discussions are approached in a practical, concrete manner. Theoretical or philosophical discussions are avoided in a business environment.

**Applications-first**  Individuals have been trained to first develop the theory or complex concept before presenting a fact, statement, or opinion. The preference is to begin a message or report by building up a theoretical argument before moving on to a conclusion. The conceptual principles underlying each situation are valued.

Netherlands. Latin American and Germanic cultures are considerably more principles-first than the United States but much less so than their Latin European cousins, so we put them around the middle of the scale. France, Russia, and Belgium appear on the principles-first side of the scale.

As always, remember the importance of cultural relativity. Where a given country falls on the scale matters less than where two cultures fall relative to one another. The British tilt rather far toward the applications-first end of the scale. But Yasser Tawfik, an Egyptian manager for Merck Pharmaceuticals, has this to say about his experience of studying in both the United Kingdom and the United States:

In the U.K., the learning was all about concept. Only after we struggled through the theoretical did we get to the practical application. The U.S. was exactly the opposite. Even before I

attended a course I was already given a case study as pre-work—
an example of practical application. In the classroom it was all
about the three Ls of leadership or the six Cs of customer satis-
faction. From moment one, we were immersed in practical solutions and examples of how to apply the solutions.

Compared with other European cultures, the United Kingdom is
quite applications-first. But when the United Kingdom is measured
against the United States, it appears strongly principles-first—a
vivid illustration of the power of cultural relativity to shape our
perceptions.

(You may be wondering where the Asian cultures fall on the
Persuading scale, since they don't appear in the diagram. Actually,
the view of the world most common in Asian cultures is so different from that of European-influenced cultures that an entirely different frame of reference, unrelated to the Persuading scale, comes
into play. We'll discuss that uniquely Asian perspective later in
this chapter.)

## WHEN PHILOSOPHY MEETS BUSINESS

Different cultures have different systems for learning in part because of the philosophers who influenced the approach to intellectual life in general and science in particular. Although Aristotle,
a Greek, is credited with articulating applications-first thinking
(induction), it was British thinkers, including Roger Bacon in the
thirteenth century and Francis Bacon in the sixteenth century, who
popularized these methodologies among modern scholars and
scientists. Later, Americans, with their pioneer mentality and dis-
inclination toward theoretical learning, came to be even more applications-first than the British.

By contrast, philosophy on the European continent has been largely driven by principles-first approaches. In the seventeenth century, Frenchman René Descartes spelled out a method of principles-first reasoning in which the scientist first formulates a hypothesis, then seeks evidence to prove or disprove it. Descartes was deeply skeptical of data based on mere observation and sought a deeper understanding of underlying principles. In the nineteenth century, the German Friedrich Hegel introduced the *dialectic* model of deduction, which reigns supreme in schools in Latin and Germanic countries. The Hegelian dialectic begins with a thesis, or foundational argument; this is opposed by an antithesis, or conflicting argument; and the two are then reconciled in a synthesis.

Clear examples of applications-first and principles-first reasoning styles can also be found in the legal systems of different societies. The British and American systems are based on common law, in which a judgment in one case sets a precedent for future cases—a clear example of applications-first thinking.

By contrast, most European Union states use the civil law system that originated in Roman law and the Napoleonic Code, in which a general statute or principle is applied on a case-by-case basis, mirroring the principles-first approach. Interestingly, Scandinavia uses a hybrid legal system that does not fall neatly into either camp. Note the middle position of the Nordic countries on the Persuading scale.

As we've seen, the way different societies analyze the world depends on their philosophical roots. These, in turn, define how we learn in school and how we behave as adults at work. It's what Frenchman Stéphane Baron realized when he found his highly persuasive writing was not having much effect on his British colleagues. A graduate of the prestigious Polytechnique engineering school, now on the fast track at a large French industrial company,

Baron was working for Michelin in Clermont Ferrand, France, as part of a global team whose other members were located mainly in the United Kingdom. Baron recalls:

> My British colleagues were not reading many of my e-mails, especially the most important ones. It was starting to annoy me. I liked my British colleagues a lot, and when we were face-to-face we had a great connection. But I had multiple indications that, when I sent e-mails to my team, they simply didn't read them. And I knew the British were big e-mail writers themselves, so I didn't think it could be cultural.

For example, Baron recalls carefully crafting a persuasive e-mail written to propose a number of key changes to company processes. The structure of his message looked something like this:

> Paragraph 1: introduced the topic.
> Paragraph 2: built up his argument, appealing to his teammates' sense of logic and developing the general principle.
> Paragraph 3: addressed the most obvious potential concerns with Baron's argument.
> Paragraph 4: explained Baron's conclusion and asked for his teammates' support.

Well educated in one of the most principles-first cultures in the world, Baron instinctively followed the dialectic method so carefully taught in the French school system. Notice how his second, third, and fourth paragraphs neatly present the thesis, antithesis, and synthesis Baron developed after much pondering of his topic.

On reflection, however, it's pretty obvious why Baron's British colleagues did not read this e-mail. Raised on the applications-first principle of *Get to the point quickly and stick to it*, they got through paragraph one and, seeing no clear point up front, moved the e-mail message to their "read at some undefined date in the future" file.

If Kara Williams and Stéphane Baron had a better understanding of the applications-first and principles-first cultural tendencies, they would each have had the chance to be a good deal more persuasive.

If Williams had realized she was presenting to an audience of principles-first Germans, perhaps she would have begun by presenting the parameters of her study and explaining why she chose this specific study method. She might then have introduced specific data to show her reasoning before presenting conclusions and recommendations. She wouldn't have needed to spend thirty minutes building her argument; five solid minutes describing her method before jumping to her results would probably have created a lot of buy-in. In addition, if Williams had recognized the crucial role of the antithesis—the counterargument—in the deductive process, she might have welcomed the challenges from her audience as a sign of interest instead of a lack of respect.

Similarly, if Baron had realized he was writing for a group raised on applications-first approaches, perhaps he would have started his e-mail with a few bullet points summarizing his proposal and explaining what he needed from the group. He might then have continued with a bit of background data, presented briskly with the recognition that "shorter is sweeter" for people with an applications-first orientation.

Baron subsequently learned this lesson. "One British colleague told me that, if my e-mail doesn't fit on the screen of an iPhone, it risks not getting read," Baron laughs. "That's the test I use now before I send out my e-mail."

The moral is clear. Presenting to Londoners or New Yorkers? Get to the point and stick to it. Presenting to French, Spaniards, or Germans? Spend more time setting the parameters and explaining the background before jumping to your conclusion.

## STRATEGIES FOR PERSUADING ACROSS CULTURES

Effective leadership often relies on the ability to persuade others to change their systems, adopt new methods of working, or adjust to new trends in markets, technologies, or business models. So if you are a manager of a team whose members come from a culture different from your own, learning to adapt your persuasive technique to your audience can be crucial.

Jorge Da Silva, a Brazilian engineer with a steel company headquartered in southern Brazil, explains how he learned to use a different approach when seeking to influence a new team of colleagues located in Houston, Texas:

> We had developed a new method for monitoring safety risks in our plants that was working beautifully and required less oversight than the status quo. Our Latin American offices were in the process of adopting the new method, but our U.S. office was resisting. They felt the method they used worked fine.
>
> We kept trying to explain to them *why* the new process was so important. However, we didn't seem to be persuading them. So we developed a very detailed presentation that explained, slide by slide, the key concepts addressed in the new method. But the more detailed we became, the less responsive our American teammates were.
>
> Finally, I called one of my colleagues in the U.S., Jake Kuderlee. I went to undergraduate school with Jake in São Paulo and have

had a great relationship with him for years. Jake asked, "Have you tried showing the decision-makers in the American office an example of what could happen if the new process is well implemented?"

Based on this discussion, we invited two of the American decision-makers to our Brazilian plant to witness how the new safety process worked. We took two days to show them around the plant, to have them interview the workers on the assembly lines, and to review the production reports. They got a really good look at the process in action, and they asked a lot of questions. And when they got back to the U.S., they got the ball rolling. Now we have the same safety process in the U.S. that we have in Brazil.

I learned my lesson. What is persuasive in Brazil may not be persuasive in an American environment.

As Da Silva learned, applications-first thinkers like to receive practical examples up front; they will extract learning from these examples. In the same vein, applications-first learners are used to the "case method," whereby they first read a case study describing a real-life story about a business problem and its solution, and then induce general lessons from it.

Principles-first thinkers also like practical examples, but they prefer to understand the basis of the framework before they move to the application. And for anyone raised in a principles-first culture, the American case method may seem downright odd. One Spanish executive told me, "In Spain, we have had it drilled into us since we were young that every situation is different and you can't assume that what happens in one situation will happen in another. So, when we are supposed to review the situation of one specific protagonist and extract general learning points, it may feel not just weird but even a bit dumb."

Shifting your persuasive style to match the preferences of your audience can be a bit challenging. However, it is still more complicated to choose the best approach if you have Brazilians, Americans, Germans, and French all attending the same presentation. As Jens Hupert, the German manager working with Kara Williams in the automotive industry, says, "My reality today is no longer a neat group of American or Germans but a large mix of participants from around the world."

The best strategy for managers in Jens's situation is to cycle back and forth between theoretical principles and practical examples. Provide practical examples to capture the interest of your applications-first listeners. The principles-first participants will enjoy them also. But you may find the latter asking theoretical questions, and, while you are answering them, the applications-first learners get bored. Try ignoring their boredom for a moment. Avoid the temptation to push away conceptual questions, as you risk sacrificing the interest and respect of your principles-first audience. Instead, take the time to answer the questions well and then quickly provide a couple of practical examples to recapture the waning attention of the applications-first students.

You may find that, no matter how well you shuttle back and forth, it will be difficult to satisfy all of your listeners all of the time. But if you are aware of the Persuading scale and the challenges it presents, you can read the cues from your audience more clearly and react accordingly.

The same differences that make it hard to persuade a multicultural audience can also make it difficult to improve collaboration among members of a multicultural team. Such teams are often much slower to make decisions than monocultural ones, and, if you consider the Persuading scale for a moment, it is easy to see why. If some team members are using principles-first logic and others are using applications-first logic to reach a decision, this can lead to conflict and inefficiency from the beginning. To make matters worse, most people have little understanding about the logic pattern they use, which leads them to judge the logic patterns of others negatively.

If the performance of your global team is suffering because its members are operating at different ends of the Persuading scale, consider the following strategies:

- Build team awareness by explaining the scale. Have everybody read this chapter and discuss it during a team meeting.
- A cultural bridge can help a lot. If you have team members who are bicultural or have significant experience living in different cultures, ask them to take responsibility for helping other team members.
- Understand and adapt to one another's behaviors.
- Patience and flexibility are key. Cross-cultural effectiveness takes time. Developing your own ability to recognize others' reactions and adapt accordingly will help you to be increasingly persuasive (and therefore effective) when working internationally.

## HOLISTIC THINKING: THE ASIAN APPROACH TO PERSUASION

Across Western countries, we see strong differences between applications-first and principles-first patterns of thinking. But when considering the differences between Asian and Western thought patterns, we need to use a different lens. Asians have what we refer to as *holistic* thought patterns, while Westerners tend to have what we will call a *specific* approach.

I ran into the Chinese holistic pattern while teaching a course for a group of seventeen top-level Chinese executives, preparing them to work in Europe. They came from different Chinese companies and different regions of China. Four were women. Six lived in Poland, Hungary, and the Netherlands, and the rest in China. Although some spoke English, I taught the session through simultaneous translation into Mandarin.

I started by covering the Communicating, Leading, and Trusting scales (the latter two of which we'll discuss later in this book). The audience was so enthusiastic that they took photos of the classroom and my slides and even recorded video clips on their iPhones. I then asked them to break out into groups to discuss how they might handle different attitudes about confrontation on a global team consisting of French and Germans (who see confrontation as a key aspect of the decision-making process) and Chinese (who see confrontation as an affront to team relationships). They discussed the issue animatedly in their separate rooms and came back to the classroom for the debriefing.

We started by asking, "What steps should the team leader in this case take to manage different attitudes toward confrontation on the team?"

Lilly Li, a bird-like woman with thick glasses and a pleasant smile who had been running operations in Hungary for two years, raised her hand:

Let me give my thoughts. In Hungary, we have people from many different countries—from all over Europe, in fact. The Trusting scale has been a big challenge for us, as the Hungarians do not take the same time to build personal relationships as we do in China. Let me explain some of the negative impact of not having a trusting relationship in our organization.

Now I was a little confused, because the question I'd asked was about confrontation, not about trusting—and there were no Hungarians in the case study we just read. I pushed the earpiece closer to my ear to make sure I was hearing the translator correctly. Lilly Li continued to talk for several minutes about trust, hierarchy, and her experiences in Hungary, and the Chinese participants listened carefully. After several long minutes of interesting comments that had—from my perspective—absolutely zero to do with the question I'd asked, Lilly Li came to the point: "In this case, if the team leader had spent more time helping the team build relationships outside of the office, that would have been very helpful during the meeting. The team would have been much more comfortable dealing with open debate and direct confrontation if the relationships on the team had been stronger."

Then another participant, Mr. Deng, raised his hand, I restated the specific question: "What steps should the team leader in this case take to manage different attitudes toward confrontation on the team?" Mr. Deng began:

> Let me give my perspective. I have been working in the technology industry for many years. In my company, we have lots of young people who are very eager and hardworking. Yet hierarchy is still strong in our company. During a meeting, if a young person is asked a question, he will look to his boss first to see if the boss's face indicates approval. If the boss approves, the younger employee will also express approval.

By now I was thinking to myself, "Mr. Deng, please don't forget the question!" After several long minutes' worth of comments about the role of hierarchy in his own organization, Mr. Deng observed, "On a global team, such as in this case, Chinese employees may confront their colleagues, but they will certainly never confront the boss. The team leader could remove himself from the meetings in order to allow for more comfortable discussions amongst his team members."

All morning long, the students' comments followed a similar pattern: After taking several minutes to discuss peripheral information, during which they would loop back to topics we had already discussed, they would then get to their point and come to a conclusion about the topic at hand. Gradually it became clear to me that this behavior did not reflect the idiosyncratic style of one person or even of one group, but rather a wider cultural norm—one that has been revealed by some of the most intriguing research in the cross-cultural field.

Professors Richard Nisbett and Takahiko Masuda presented twenty-second animated video vignettes of underwater scenes to Japanese and American participants (see an illustration of one of the vignettes in Figure 3.2 on page 108).[1] Afterward, participants were asked what they had seen, and the first sentence of each response was categorized.

The results of the study were remarkable. While the Americans mentioned larger, faster-moving, brightly colored objects in the foreground (such as the big fish visible in the illustration), the Japanese spoke more about what was going on in the background (for example, the plants or the small frog to the bottom left). In addition, the Japanese spoke twice as often as the Americans about the interdependencies between the objects up front and the objects

FIGURE 3.2

in the background. As one Japanese woman explained, "I naturally look at all the items behind and around the large fish to determine what kind of fish they are."

In a second study, Americans and Japanese were asked to "take a photo of a person." The Americans most frequently took a close-up, showing all the features of the person's face, while the Japanese showed the person in his or her environment instead, with the human figure quite small in relationship to the background (see Figure 3.3).

In a third study, Nisbett and Masuda asked American and Taiwanese students to read narratives and watch videos of silent comedies—for example, a film about a day in the life of a woman, during which circumstances conspire to prevent her from getting to work—and then to summarize them. In their summaries, the

FIGURE 3.3. Left: American portrait. Right: Japanese portrait

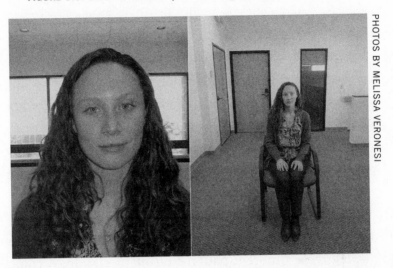

PHOTOS BY MELISSA VERONESI

Americans made about 30 percent more statements referring to the central figures of the stories than their Taiwanese counterparts did.[2]

Notice the common pattern in all three studies. The Americans focus on individual figures separate from their environment, while the Asians give more attention to backgrounds and to the links between these backgrounds and the central figures. I have found these tendencies to be borne out in my own interviews with groups of multicultural managers. While Western European and Anglo-Saxon managers generally follow the American tendencies of specific thinking patterns, East Asians respond as the Japanese and Taiwanese did in Nisbett's research.

In addition, I've often watched Westerners and Asians discuss these studies. Here's a bit of dialogue taken directly from a classroom debate about the photo study:

Western participant: But the instructions said to take a photo of a person, and the picture on the left *is* a photo of a person. The picture on the right is a photo of a room. Why would the Japanese take a photo of a room when they have been asked to take a photo of a person?

Asian participant: The photo on the left is not a photo of the person. It is a close-up of a face. How can I determine anything about the person by looking at it? The photo on the right is a photo of the person, the entire person, including surrounding elements so you can determine something about that person. Why would the Americans take a close-up of a face, which leaves out all of the important details?

Perhaps it's not surprising that Westerners and Asians tend to display these different patterns of interpretation. A common tenet of Western philosophies and religions is that you can remove an item from its environment and analyze it separately. Aristotle, for example, emphasized focusing attention on a salient object. Its properties could then be assessed and the object assigned a category with the goal of finding rules that governed its behavior. For example, looking at a piece of wood floating in water, Aristotle said that it had the property of "levity," while a stone falling through air had the property of "gravity." He referred to the wood and the rock as if each was a separate and isolated object in its own right. Cultural theorists call this *specific thinking*.

Chinese religions and philosophies, by contrast, have traditionally emphasized interdependencies and interconnectedness. Ancient Chinese thought was *holistic*, meaning that the Chinese attended to the field in which an object was located, believing that action always occurs in a field of forces that influence the action. Taoism, which influenced Buddhism and Confucianism, proposes that the universe works harmoniously, its various elements dependent upon one another. The terms *yin* and *yang* (literally "dark" and "light") describe how seemingly contrary forces are interconnected and interdependent.

With this background in mind, let's reconsider my class of seventeen Chinese executives. Here's a comment from one of the Chinese participants after we'd discussed the fish and photo research studies:

> Chinese people think from macro to micro, whereas Western people think from micro to macro. For example, when writing an address, the Chinese write in sequence of province, city, district, block, gate number. The Westerners do just the opposite— they start with the number of a single house and gradually work their way up to the city and state. In the same way, Chinese put the surname first, whereas the Westerners do it the other way around. And Chinese put the year before month and date. Again, it's the opposite in the West.

It's easy to see how these differences in the characteristic sequence of thinking may cause difficulty or misunderstanding when people from Asian and Western cultures are involved in conversation. A typical example is that Westerners may think that the Chinese are going all around the key points without addressing them deliberately, while East Asians may experience Westerners as trying to make a decision by isolating a single factor and ignoring significant interdependencies.

This difference affects how business thinking is perceived in Western and Asian cultures. In the eyes of Asian business leaders, European and American executives tend to make decisions without taking much time to consider the broader implications of their actions. As Bae Pak from the Korean motor company Kia explains, "When we work with our Western colleagues, we are often taken aback by their tendency to make decisions without considering how their decisions are impacting various business units, clients, and suppliers. We feel their decisions are hasty and often ignore the surrounding impact."

## INCREASING YOUR EFFECTIVENESS

In a *specific* culture when managing a supplier or team member, people usually respond well to receiving very detailed and segmented information about what you expect of each of them. If you need to give instructions to a team member from a specific culture, focus on what that person needs to accomplish when. If you explain clearly what you need each person to work on, that allows them to home in effectively on their specific task.

In *holistic* cultures if you need to motivate, manage, or persuade someone, you will be more influential if you take the time to explain the big picture and show how all the pieces fit together. When I interviewed Jacek Malecki, an unusually big man with a friendly round face and quiet voice, he was working for Toshiba Westinghouse. He provided this example of how he had learned to manage his staff in a more holistic manner.

> I had recently been promoted and for the first time I was managing not just Europeans and Americans but also Japanese. I have managed teams for sixteen years, and I've learned over the years to do it well. When I took my first trip to meet with my Japanese staff, I managed the objective-setting process like I always had. I called each person on the team into my office for a meeting.

During the meeting we discussed what each individual on the team should accomplish. I outlined each person's short-term and long-term goals and the individual bonus plan for meeting and exceeding expectations.

But as Malecki later realized, his approach had not worked well for his Japanese team. "If they don't understand what others are working on and how the pieces fit together, they don't feel comfortable or persuaded to move to action. Although I noticed they asked a lot of peripheral questions during the meetings, none of them actually explained to me that my approach was not ideal for them so I went back to Poland with a false sense of comfort."

When Malecki returned to Tokyo several weeks later he saw that the way he had divided up the tasks and set individual incentives didn't match the way his team was working.

The team had spent a lot of time consulting with one another about what each person had been asked to do and how their individual objectives fit together to create a big picture. The team was now making good progress but not in the way I had segmented the project. I learned that the type of specific division of tasks as well as individual incentive plans don't work well in a Japanese environment.

The lesson Malecki learned is a good one for anyone who needs to manage or influence holistic thinkers. If you need to explain a project or set objectives or sell an idea to a holistic audience, begin by explaining the big picture in detail. Outline not just the overall project but also how the parts are connected before drilling down what specifically needs to be accomplished and when.

## AVOIDING THE PITFALLS, REAPING THE BENEFITS

With words like "diversity" and "global" all the rage, many companies are seeking to create multinational, multicultural teams in an effort to reap benefits in the form of added creativity and greater understanding of global markets. However, as we've seen, cultural differences can be fraught with challenges. Effective cross-cultural collaboration can take more time than monocultural collaboration and often needs to be managed more closely. Here are two simple tips that can help you realize the benefits of such collaboration while avoiding the dangers.

First, on a multicultural team, you can save time by having as few people in the group work across cultures as possible. For example, if you are building a global team that includes small groups of participants from four countries, choose one or two people from each country—the most internationally experienced of the bunch—to do most of the cross-cultural collaborating. Meanwhile, you can leave the others to work in the local way that is most natural to them. That way, you can have the innovation from the combination of cultures, while avoiding the inefficiency that comes with the clash of cultures.

Second, think carefully about your larger objectives before you mix cultures up. If your goal is innovation or creativity, the more cultural diversity the better, as long as the process is managed carefully. But if your goal is simple speed and efficiency, then monocultural is probably better than multicultural. Sometimes, it is simply better to leave Rome to the Romans.

# 4

## How Much Respect Do You Want?

Leadership, Hierarchy, and Power

What does a good boss look like? Try to answer the question quickly without giving it much thought. When you picture the perfect leader, is he wearing a navy Armani suit and a pair of highly polished wingtips, or khaki trousers, a sweater, and comfy jogging shoes? Does she travel to work on a mountain bike or driving a black Ferrari? Is the ideal leader someone that you would naturally call "Mr. Director," or would you prefer to address him as "Sam"?

For Ulrich Jepsen, a Danish executive in his early thirties who has spent the past ten years on the management fast track working for Maersk, a Copenhagen-based multinational container-shipping company, the answer is clear:

> In Denmark, it is understood that the managing director is one of the guys, just two small steps up from the janitor. I worked hard to be the type of leader who is a facilitator among equals rather than a director giving orders from on high. I felt it was important to dress just as casually as every other member of my

team, so they didn't feel I was arrogant or consider myself to be above them.

Danes call everyone by their first name and I wouldn't feel comfortable being called anything but Ulrich. In my staff meetings, the voices of the interns and administrative assistants count as much as mine or any of the directors. This is quite common in Denmark.

Jepsen does not have an open-door policy—but only because he doesn't have a door. In fact, he chose to not have an office (they are rare in his company's headquarters). Instead, he works in an open space among his staff. If any team members need a quiet place to talk, they can slip into a nearby conference room.

Jepsen continues:

Managing Danes, I have learned that the best way to get things done is to push power down in the organization and step out of the way. That really motivates people here. I am a big fan of tools like management by objectives and 360-degree feedback, which allow me to manage the team from more or less the same level as them.

The belief that individuals should be considered equal and that individual achievement should be downplayed has been a part of Scandinavian society for centuries, but it was codified in the so-called "Law of Jante" by Danish author Aksel Sandemose in his 1933 novel *En flyktning krysser sitt spor* (A Fugitive Crosses His Tracks). Sandemose's writing was intended as a critique of Scandinavian culture as reflected in the homogeneity and repression characteristic of the fictional small town of Jante. Nonetheless, the rules of equality Sandemose described seem to be deeply etched into the Danish psyche. Jepsen observes:

> Although a lot of Danes would like to change this, we have been bathed since childhood in extreme egalitarian principles: Do not think you are better than others. Do not think you are smarter than others. Do not think you are more important than others. Do not think you are someone special. These and the other Jante rules are a very deep part of the way we live and the way we prefer to be managed.

Jepsen's egalitarian leadership style was so appreciated in Denmark that he was promoted four times in four years. But the fifth promotion put Jepsen in charge of the company's recently acquired Russian operation, his first international leadership position.

Relocated to a small town outside of Saint Petersburg, Jepsen was surprised by the difficulties he encountered in managing his team. After four months in his new job, he e-mailed me this list of complaints about his Russian staff:

1. They call me Mr. President
2. They defer to my opinions
3. They are reluctant to take initiative
4. They ask for my constant approval
5. They treat me like I am king

When Jepsen and I met to discuss his cross-cultural challenges, he provided a concrete example: "Week two into the job, our IT director e-mailed me to outline in detail a problem we were having with the e-mail process and describing various solutions. He ended his e-mail, 'Mr. President, kindly explain how you would like me to handle this.' This was the first of many such e-mails from various directors to fill my inbox. All problems are pushed up, up, up, and I do my best to nudge them way back down." After all, as Jepsen told the IT manager, "You know the situation better than I do. You are the expert, not me."

Meanwhile, the members of Jepsen's Russian management team were equally annoyed at Jepsen's apparent lack of competence as a leader. Here are some of the complaints they offered during focus group interviews:

1. He is a weak, ineffective leader
2. He doesn't know how to manage
3. He gave up his corner office on the top floor, suggesting to the company that our team is of no importance
4. He is incompetent

While Jepsen was groaning that his team members took no initiative, they were wringing their hands about Jepsen's lack of leadership: "We are just waiting for a little bit of direction!"

How about you? Do you prefer an egalitarian or a hierarchical management approach? No matter what your nationality, the answer is probably the same. Most people throughout the world claim to prefer an egalitarian style, and a large majority of managers say that they use an egalitarian approach themselves.

But evidence from the cross-cultural trenches shows another story. When people begin managing internationally, their day-to-day work reveals quite different preferences—and these unexpected, unconscious differences can make leading across cultures surprisingly difficult, as a Mexican manager named Carlos Gomez discovered when his work for the Heineken brewing company brought him a continent away, to Amsterdam.

Teaching a group of Heineken managers feels at first a little like entering a sports bar. The classroom walls are covered with advertisements for various beer brands and there are life-size cardboard cutouts of cocktail waitresses serving up a cold one as you enter the room. Given the overall spirit of relaxed friendliness, I was half expecting the participants to lurch into a round of the Dutch drinking song "In de Hemel is Geen Bier" (In Heaven There Is No Beer) as I started my session.

Heineken, of course, is a Dutch brewing company with a market presence in seventy countries. If you like beer, it's likely you know one of the international Heineken brands, not only the eponymous Heineken but also Amstel, Moretti, or Kingfisher. When you visit Heineken's headquarters in Amsterdam, in addition to finding a beer-tasting museum around the corner, you will find a lot of tall blond Dutch people and also a lot of . . . Mexicans. In 2010, Heineken purchased a big operation in Monterrey, Mexico, and now a large number of Heineken employees come from northeastern Mexico.

One is Carlos Gomez, and as our session began, he described to the class his experiences since moving to Amsterdam a year earlier.

"It is absolutely incredible to manage Dutch people and nothing like my experience leading Mexican teams," Gomez said, "because the Dutch do not care at all who is the boss in the room."

At this, Gomez's Dutch colleagues began breaking into knowing laughter. But Gomez protested:

Don't laugh! It's not funny. I struggle with this every day. I will schedule a meeting in order to roll out a new process, and during the meeting my team starts challenging the process, taking the meeting in various unexpected directions, ignoring my process altogether, and paying no attention to the fact that they work for me. Sometimes I just watch them astounded. Where is the respect?

You guys know me. You know I am not a tyrant or a dictator, and I believe as deeply in the importance of leveraging creativity from every member of the team as any Dutch person in this room. But in the culture where I was born and raised and have spent my entire life, we give more respect to someone who is senior to us. We show a little more deference to the person in charge.

Yes, you can say we are more hierarchical. And I don't know how to lead a team if my team does not treat me as their boss, but simply one of them. It is confusing for me, because the way they treat me makes me want to assert my authority more vigorously than I would ever want or need to do in Mexico. But I know that is exactly the wrong approach.

I know this treating everyone as pure equals is the Dutch way, so I keep quiet and try to be patient. But often I just feel like getting down on my knees and pleading with them, "Dear colleagues, in case you have forgotten—I . . . am . . . the boss."

## GEERT HOFSTEDE AND THE CONCEPT OF POWER DISTANCE

Carlos Gomez finds managing a team of workers from Holland terribly frustrating because of the enormous gap between Mexican and Dutch cultures when it comes to power distance. This concept grew out of an ocean journey taken at the age of eighteen by Geert Hofstede, who would eventually become the most famous cross-cultural researcher in history.

Hofstede traveled to Indonesia as an assistant engineer on a ship and was struck by the cultural differences between the people of Indonesia and his fellow Dutchmen. Later, when he got to know an English woman on a different voyage, he realized that strong cultural differences can exist even between countries that are geographically close. These differences fascinated Hofstede. Eventually, as a professor of social psychology, Hofstede was the first person to use significant research data to map world cultures on scales.

Hofstede developed the term "power distance" while analyzing 100,000 management surveys at IBM in the 1970s. He defined power distance as "the extent to which the less powerful members of organizations accept and expect that power is distributed unequally." Hofstede also looked at power distance in families and in various other social structures, such as tribes or communities.[1]

In a more recent study, a group of academic scholars from around the world led by Professor Robert House conducted thousands of interviews across sixty-two countries during which they tested and calibrated Hofstede's data on the power distance scales again.[2] This project is often referred to as the Globe Project. House and his colleagues looked at the degree to which inequality in a society is both supported and desired and considered the impact on egalitarian versus hierarchical leadership preferences in various countries.

The Leading scale takes Hofstede's idea of power distance and applies it specifically to business. Power distance relates to questions like:

- How much respect or deference is shown to an authority figure?
- How god-like is the boss?

- Is it acceptable to skip layers in your company? If you want to communicate a message to someone two levels above or below you, should you go through the hierarchical chain?
- When you are the boss, what gives you an aura of authority?

As the last question in this list suggests, power distance is related, in part, to the signals that are used to mark power within an organization or other social group. Such signals, of course, may be interpreted very differently in different parts of the world. Behavior that shouts "This man has the leadership skills to move mountains and motivate armies" in one society may squeak "This man has the leadership skills of a three-footed mouse" in another.

In an egalitarian culture, for example, an aura of authority is more likely to come from acting like one of the team, while in a hierarchical culture, an aura of authority tends to come from setting yourself clearly apart.

I met Anne-Hélène Gutierres when she was the teaching assistant in my advanced French course at the University of Minnesota. I sat behind her in class, admired her long smooth brown hair and her lightly accented English, and tried to imagine what it would be like to leave the Parisian City of Lights for the long, cold winters of midwestern America.

As luck would have it, I bumped into Gutierres again years later, when we had both moved to Paris. She told me about some of the surprising things she had encountered while working at a small Minneapolis-based consulting firm—her first job outside of France.

One morning Gutierres arrived at work to find her computer wasn't working. As she had an important presentation to finish, she turned to her American colleagues for advice. She recalls: "Imagine my surprise when they responded, 'Pam isn't here today, why don't you use her computer? She won't mind. She has an open door policy.' Pam was the president of the company!"

Gutierres still remembers the feeling of opening up the big glass door to Pam's office, approaching her desk, and touching the keyboard. "Even though Pam was out of the country, I could feel the power of her position hovering over that space. Later, when I told my French friends about the experience, we all laughed trying to imagine how our French bosses might react if they knew we had made ourselves comfortable sitting in their chairs and using their things."

Gutierres's story suggests the aura of authority that surrounds the material possessions of a boss in French culture. More broadly, it suggests the important role symbols play in defining power distance. Thus, if you are the boss, your behavior may be speaking volumes without your even recognizing it.

Take a simple action like riding a bike to work. In countries like Jepsen's Denmark, when the boss rides a bike to work (which is common), it may symbolize to the egalitarian Danes a strong leadership voice: "Look, I'm one of you." Something similar applies in Australia, as explained by Steve Henning, an executive in the textile industry:

> One of my most proud lifestyle choices back in Australia was the fact that I was a near-full-time bicycle commuter. My Surly Long Haul Trucker bike wasn't just a toy; it was a fully equipped workhorse that was used for shopping, getting around, traveling to and from work, weekend leisure rides, and anything else I needed.
>
> I'm a senior vice president in our company, and my Australian staff thought it was great that I rode a bike to work. If anything,

they liked that their boss showed up to work in a bike helmet. So I decided to bring my bicycle with me when I was assigned to a new job in China.

Henning had been using his bike during his daily commute in Beijing for a while when he discovered that the tactic had certainly attracted attention from his team members. "Just not the type of attention I was hoping for," Henning sighs. While sharing a dinner and drinks with a Chinese colleague and friend, Henning learned what his staff was saying about him:

> My team was humiliated that their boss rode a bike to work like a common person. While Chinese bike to work infinitely more than Australians, among the wealthier Chinese, bikes are not an option. There are plenty of bikes on the road, but biking is for the lower classes only.
>
> So my team felt it was an embarrassment that their boss rode a bike to the office. They felt it suggested to the entire company that their boss was unimportant, and that by association, they were unimportant, too.
>
> Well, I love my bike, but I was in China to get my team motivated and on track. I certainly didn't want to sabotage my success just to arrive sweaty at the office every morning. I gave up the bike and started taking public transportation, just like every other Chinese boss.

Once you understand the power distance messages your actions are sending, you can make an informed choice about what behaviors to change. But if you don't know what your behaviors signify, you'll have no control over the signals you send—and the results can be disastrous.

## HISTORICAL AND CULTURAL FACTORS THAT
## AFFECT THE LEADING SCALE

Our placement of cultures on the Leading scale, which positions cultures from highly egalitarian to strongly hierarchical (Figure 4.1), draws heavily on Hofstede's work and the Globe Project research. It also incorporates data from my own work with hundreds of international executives. On the scale and from now on we'll use the word *egalitarian* instead of *low power distance* and *hierarchical* instead of *high power distance.*

A glance at the Leading scale reveals a number of interesting and important anomalies.

One relates to the placement of European cultures on the scale. Once, while doing some work for an Ohio-based food producer, I worked with a group of executives who frequently sold products and services via telephone to clients from many countries. When I spoke to the participants on the phone during my planning for our

### FIGURE 4.1. **LEADING**

| Denmark | Israel | Canada | US | | | France | Poland | Saudi Arabia | Japan |
| Netherlands | | Finland | UK | Germany | Italy | | Russia | India | Korea |
| Sweden | Australia | | | Brazil | Spain | Mexico | Peru | China | Nigeria |

**Egalitarian** ←————————————————————————→ **Hierarchical**

**Egalitarian**  The ideal distance between a boss and a subordinate is low. The best boss is a facilitator among equals. Organizational structures are flat. Communication often skips hierarchical lines.

**Hierarchical**  The ideal distance between a boss and a subordinate is high. The best boss is a strong director who leads from the front. Status is important. Organizational structures are multilayered and fixed. Communication follows set hierarchical lines.

session, several told me that they would like to learn more about the "European culture."

Take a good look at the Leading scale and see if you can identify the location of "European culture." As your eye scans from Denmark and Sweden on the extreme left of the scale all the way down to Italy and Spain in the middle-right, you'll realize that what it means to be "culturally European" on this scale is not very evident. Although Europe is a small geographical area, it embraces large differences in opinion about what it means to be a good boss.

These variations within Europe have been examined by a number of different researchers. For example, in the 1980s, 1990s, and early 2000s, my colleague Professor André Laurent polled hundreds of European managers about a number of leadership issues.[3] One of the questions he asked was, "Is it important for a manager to have at hand precise answers to most of the questions subordinates may raise about their work?"

Take a look (Figure 4.2) at the percentages of respondents from each country who responded "yes" to this question:

As you can see, the answers varied dramatically from one nationality to the next. While 55 percent of Italians polled claimed that it is important for the boss to have most of the answers, only 7 percent of Swedes thought the same way. In recent follow-up interviews, Swedish managers explained that a conscious approach to leadership underlies this attitude. One commented, "Even if I know the answer, I probably won't give it to my staff . . . because I want them to figure it out for themselves." An Italian manager would be more likely to say, "If I don't provide my people with the answers they need, how can they move ahead?"

Intrigued by these results, Professor Laurent puzzled over the historic factors that might have pushed these various European cultures to have such different identities when it comes to the role

**FIGURE 4.2.**

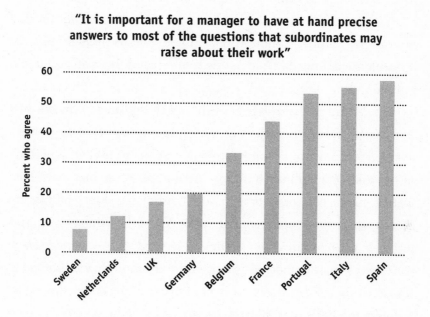

"It is important for a manager to have at hand precise
answers to most of the questions that subordinates may
raise about their work"

of the boss. Here are three clues you might recall from your high
school history classes.

The first clue is one I recall from my tenth-grade teacher, Mr.
Duncan, who told our class about how the Roman Empire swept
across southern Europe. He recounted in hushed tones how the
Romans built hierarchical social and political structures and heavily centralized systems for managing their vast empire. The boundaries between the different classes were strict and legally enforced.
Members of different classes even dressed differently. Only the
emperor was allowed to wear a purple toga, while senators could
wear a white toga with a broad purple stripe along the edge, and
equestrians, who ranked just below the senators, wore togas with
a narrow purple stripe. The class of the person was therefore no-
ticeable at first glimpse.

So a first historical point is that the countries that fell under the influence of the Roman Empire (including Spain, Italy, and, to a lesser degree, France) tend to be more hierarchical than the rest of Western Europe. Although your Italian boss is unlikely to wear a purple toga, invisible and subtle remnants of these attitudes still remain today.

The second clue relates to a much later European empire, one that dominated the northern part of the continent to almost as great an extent as the Roman Empire dominated the south. When you think of the Vikings, you may think of hulking muscular men with long walrus mustaches and hats with horns, riding big ships and waging bloody wars. What you may not know is that the Vikings were surprisingly egalitarian. When settling in Iceland, they founded one of the world's early democracies. The entire community was invited to the debating hall to thrash out the hot topics of the day, followed by a vote, with each person's opinion carrying equal weight. Legend has it that, when the Prince of Franks sent an envoy from southern Europe to negotiate with the Vikings, the puzzled envoy returned confused and disheartened, complaining, "I couldn't figure out who to talk with. They said they were all the chiefs."

The countries most influenced by the Vikings consistently rank as some of the most egalitarian and consensus-oriented cultures in the world today. So it is no surprise that, even today, when you walk into a meeting room in Copenhagen or Stockholm, it is often impossible to spot the boss.

Our third historical clue relates to the distance between the people and God in particular religions. Countries with Protestant cultures tend to fall further to the egalitarian side of the scale than those with a more Catholic tradition. One interpretation of this pattern is that the Protestant Reformation largely removed the traditional hierarchy from the church. In many strains of Protestantism, the individual speaks directly to God instead of speaking to God through the priest, the bishop, and the pope. Thus, it's natural that societies in which Protestant religions predominate tend to be more egalitarian than those dominated by Catholicism.

Of course, all three of these historical observations are dramatic oversimplifications, as each country has a rich and complex history that helps shape its leadership beliefs. But even in this day of text messaging and video calls, where cross-cultural interactions are commonplace, events that took place thousands of years ago continue to influence the cultures in which individuals are raised and formed—and these historical forces help to explain why European countries appear in such widely different locations on the Leading scale.

Meanwhile, a glance to the right-hand side of the scale, where hierarchical countries are clustered, reveals a large number of Asian cultures. Here, again, we can point to a significant historical influence that helps to explain this pattern—the ancient Chinese philosopher Confucius.

When I was in my teens, my family had a Chinese doctoral student named Ronan living with us one winter in Minneapolis. My older brother and I were often fighting, and after one of our disagreements, Ronan told me the story of Kong Rong, who was a Han Dynasty scholar, politician, and warlord. According to Ronan, when Kong Rong was four years old, he was given the opportunity to choose a pear from among several. Instead of taking the largest pear, he took the smallest pear, saying that the larger pears should be eaten by his older brothers. Although the story did nothing to change my feelings toward my brother, the oddity of the message stuck in my mind. I didn't much like pears, but I certainly wouldn't give the nicest one to my brother just because he happened to be born two years before me.

Obviously, I wasn't raised with Confucian principles. But in Confucian Asia, the older sibling is clearly positioned above the younger one. Thus, in Chinese families, children are generally not spoken to in the family by their personal names but rather by their kinship titles ("Older sister," "2nd brother," "4th sister," and so on). In this way, they are constantly reminded of their position in the family relative to everyone else's.

Confucius was mainly interested in how to bring about societal order and harmony. He believed that mankind would be in harmony with the universe if everyone understood their rank in society and observed the behaviors proper to that rank. Accordingly, he believed that the social order was threatened whenever people failed to act according to their prescribed roles. Confucius devised a system of interdependent relationships, a sort of structure in which the lower level gives obedience to the higher, while those who are higher protect and mentor the lower. The structure, which he called *wu lun*, outlined five principal relationships:

Emperor (kindness) over Subject (loyalty)
Father (protection) over Son (respect and obedience)
Husband (obligation) over Wife (submission)
Older Brother (care) over Younger Brother (model subject)
Senior Friends (trust) over Junior Friends (trust)

If Confucius were alive today and updated his model for today's business leaders, he would likely add a sixth human relationship to his structure: Boss (kindness, protection, care) over Subordinate (loyalty, respect, obedience).

To this day, perhaps because of their Confucian heritage, East Asian societies, from China to South Korea to Japan, have a paternalistic view of leadership that is puzzling to Westerners. In this kind of "father knows best" society, the patriarch sitting at the top of the pyramid rarely has his views or ideas challenged. And though Asian countries have begun to move past these narrowly defined roles in politics, business, and daily life, due in part to growing influence from the West, most Asians today are still used to thinking in terms of hierarchy. They tend to respect hierarchy and differences in status much more than Westerners.

In egalitarian cultures, the down-to-earth CEO who chats with the janitor every morning on a first-name basis is often singled out for praise. You won't see this in China or Korea.

Some of the main points to remember about egalitarian versus hierarchical cultures are summarized in Figure 4.3.

**FIGURE 4.3.**

| General traits of egalitarian cultures: | General traits of hierarchical cultures: |
|---|---|
| It's okay to disagree with the boss openly even in front of others. | An effort is made to defer to the boss's opinion especially in public. |
| People are more likely to move to action without getting the boss's okay. | People are more likely to get the boss's approval before moving to action. |
| If meeting with a client or supplier, there is less focus on matching hierarchical levels. | If you send your boss, they will send their boss. If your boss cancels, their boss also may not come. |
| It's okay to e-mail or call people several levels below or above you. | Communication follows the hierarchical chain. |
| With clients or partners you will be seated and spoken to in no specific order. | With clients or partners you may be seated and spoken to in order of position. |

## LEARNING TO MANAGE IN A HIERARCHICAL CULTURE

Like any good American, I was raised to be quite uncomfortable with the idea of a fixed social hierarchy. When I thought of hierarchy, I thought of the lowest person's responsibility to obey, which I felt suggested an inhumane situation, like a relationship between slave and owner. I saw this as being in direct contrast to individual freedom.

However, in order to understand the Confucian concept of hierarchy, it is important to think not just about the lower level person's responsibility to obey, but also about the heavy responsibility of the higher person to protect and care for those under him. The leader's responsibility for caring and teaching is just as strong as the follower's responsibility to defer and follow directions. Those from Confucian societies have believed for centuries that this type of dual responsibility is the backbone of a virtuous society.

Recognizing and respecting this system of reciprocal obligations is important for the manager from an egalitarian society who finds himself working with a team from a hierarchical society, particularly one from Asia. Like a good Confucian, you must remember your obligations. Your team may follow your instructions to the letter, but in return, you must show a consistent paternalistic kindness. Protect your subordinates, mentor and coach them, behave as a kind father would to his children, and always look out for their interests. Play your role well, and you may find that leading a team in a hierarchical culture brings many rewards.

After several years in China, Steve Henning, the Australian bike rider we met earlier in the chapter, summarized his own experience:

What a pleasure to lead a Chinese team! When I was managing in Europe, every idea I tried to implement had to be hashed out at each level of the department. Hours and hours were lost trying to create buy-in. When I first started working here in China, I felt frustrated that my staff wouldn't push back or challenge my ideas in the way I was used to. But I have developed a very close relationship with my team members over the past six years—almost a father-son connection. And I have come to love managing in China. There is great beauty in giving a clear instruction and watching your competent and enthusiastic team willingly attack the project without pushing back or challenging.

As we've noted, symbolic gestures can send important signals about the style of leadership you practice. This is why the use of names is significant. Many Western managers, who tend to prefer informal, egalitarian relationships, try to get their Asian subordinates to call them by their first names. However, if the age and status gap is wide, most will be uncomfortable doing so. You'll have better luck suggesting they call you by a hybrid name/title— something like "Mr. Mike."

Similarly, details of etiquette may prove critical to your success in China, Korea, or Japan. When you enter a room, you should know whose hand to shake first (the boss's) and with whom to exchange pleasantries before sitting down to serious business (everyone in descending hierarchical order). When hosting a dinner, you should make seating arrangements according to the rankings of your guests, lest you offend someone. Get any of these details wrong, and you risk not making it to the next meeting, let alone closing the deal.

## LEVEL-HOPPING: LOOK BEFORE YOU JUMP

No matter which country you work in, there is a PowerPoint slide buried somewhere in the human resources department that shows the organizational structure of your company. Your own name is located somewhere on the chart in a neat box, and if you follow the lines up from that box you will see the name of your boss, above that the name of your boss's boss, and eventually the name of the chairman of the company. If you follow the lines down, you will see those who report to you listed in a neat line, and those who report to those people in neat lines below that one. This kind of on-paper hierarchy is common to every business culture—but the appropriate ways to navigate it in the real world differ widely, depending on how hierarchical or egalitarian that culture is.

For example, what if you would like to speak to someone who is not just one level above you (your direct boss) but someone who is several levels above you? Can you simply pick up the phone and dial that person's number, or drop in to the corner office for a quick meeting and a cup of coffee? If you do this, how will the boss of bosses respond—and what will your direct boss think?

The answer may depend in part on the type of company you work for and the specific personalities involved. But cultural differences may play an even greater role.

In more egalitarian cultures, it is often acceptable for communication to skip organizational levels. Carlos Gomez, the Mexican manager working in the Netherlands for Heineken, had this to say:

> I had two educational experiences shortly after my move. First, my new administrative assistant, Karl de Groot, was grabbing his coat to head out for lunch. I asked him if he wanted to get a

sandwich with me, and he casually mentioned that he couldn't because he was having lunch with Jan, who is incidentally the general manager of our operation and my boss's boss. Apparently they had met in the elevator and Karl had suggested they have lunch. I was a little dumbfounded that an administrative assistant would set up a meeting with his boss's boss's boss without asking anyone's okay or even informing his direct supervisor—me!

Gomez asked his Dutch colleagues what they thought about this incident, and everyone seemed to think it was perfectly normal, so he shrugged it off. Then, during a staff meeting a couple of weeks later, a second incident occurred:

One of my direct reports, a smart, ambitious manager who has really good people skills, mentioned casually that he had just e-mailed the CEO of the company with some criticism about a new initiative. He announced it to the entire team like it was the most normal thing in the world that he would e-mail someone who has over 64,000 employees and is five levels above him, without even telling me—his direct boss—or anyone else.

Sometimes when I'm uncomfortable, I feel my smile spread and freeze across my face, and this was one of those times. I actively worked on keeping my lips firmly closed because I understood that, in a Dutch cultural environment, this was acceptable, but I wanted to say, "You did what?!" I felt my pulse racing just thinking about what kind of scolding I would be getting from the big boss the next time I was in a meeting with him about this loose cannon on my team.

Of course, that never happened, as he is also . . . well, Dutch.

The fact that all the people involved in these two stories lived and worked in the same environment made it a little easier for Gomez to process the cultural challenge involved. Over time, Gomez had become increasingly aware of what was appropriate in a Dutch cultural environment, so he was able to wrestle with his reactions in order to respond appropriately. The challenge of level-hopping can be even more complicated when the individuals involved are living and working in different countries, as may happen when long-distance communication via phone, e-mail, or another electronic medium is used.

I was once asked to help improve the collaboration between two teams, one in Vancouver and one in Bangalore. Sarah Peterson, the manager of the Vancouver team, had eight Canadians working for her. "We develop the specifications for the software our clients need, and we send it to Bangalore where Rishi Rangan's team of about twenty-five programmers complete the work," she explained.

"The problem began a few months ago when I needed information from one of the programmers on Rishi's staff, and I e-mailed that person asking for information. No response. Three follow-up e-mails. Still no answer. Later, I needed something from another person on Rishi's team, but again when I e-mailed her, no reply."

Peterson was fed up. "We pay these guys good money to do this work for us. So I called Rishi to complain about the lack of communication from his team." But the situation did not improve. "It's an incredible waste of time!"

In hopes of diagnosing the cause of the problem, I phoned Rangan. "I honestly don't know what I have done to break trust with Sarah," he sighed. "But things have become so bad between us now that she is unwilling to work with me."

I asked the soft-spoken Rangan to explain what had happened. And what I heard was a very different interpretation of the situation than the one I had heard from Sarah Peterson:

> Sarah e-mails my staff directly. She seems to purposefully circumnavigate me. I am the manager: she should e-mail me, not my staff. Of course, when my team members receive these e-mails, they are paralyzed by the fact that someone at her level would e-mail them directly. They certainly don't want to be brought into this issue between her and me. And then she complains that we are poor communicators!

As this story illustrates, although e-mail is a relatively recent technological tool, different societies have already developed radically different patterns for using it. Because the two software teams in this case had misunderstood one another so badly, it was necessary to convene an in-person meeting between the groups to iron out their differences. "The trip was expensive. It's not cheap to fly nine people from Vancouver to Bangalore for a three-day meeting," Peterson later reflected. "But while together, we discussed our perceptions, cultural differences, and expectations, and we were able to improve the situation—to get back to page one."

When all is said and done, humans are flexible. Most of the time, if managers take extra pains up front to discuss how they are going to communicate, many painful and costly faux pas can be avoided entirely. The problem comes when both parties proceed, as Rangan and Peterson did, as if their style was normal and the other party was wrong. Once they understood the other's behavior, things moved along well. Peterson readily agreed to copy

Rangan on all her e-mails in the future. And Rangan agreed that it would be fine for her to go straight to his staff with urgent requests: He would let them know the new protocol immediately.

Here are some simple strategies for cross-cultural level-skipping that can help you avoid the kinds of problems that Rangan and Peterson encountered. If you are working with people from a hierarchical society:

- Communicate with the person at your level. If you are the boss, go through the boss with equivalent status, or get explicit permission to hop from one level to another.
- If you do e-mail someone at a lower hierarchical level than your own, copy the boss.
- If you need to approach your boss's boss or your subordinate's subordinate, get permission from the person at the level in between first.
- When e-mailing, address the recipient by the last name unless they have indicated otherwise—for example, by signing their e-mail to you with their first name only.

If you are working with people from an egalitarian society:

- Go directly to the source. No need to bother the boss.
- Think twice before copying the boss. Doing so could suggest to the recipient that you don't trust them or are trying to get them in trouble.
- Skipping hierarchical levels probably won't be a problem.
- In Scandinavia, the Netherlands, and Australia, use first names when writing e-mails. This is also largely true for the United States and the United Kingdom, although regional and circumstantial differences may arise.

If you aren't sure about where the culture you're working with falls on this scale, follow the hierarchical recommendations, which are generally safer and unlikely to get you into trouble accidentally. And if you are leading a global team, with members of various cultures with different positions on the Leading scale, define team protocols up front. When do we skip levels? Whom do we copy and when? Most misunderstandings can be avoided by defining a clear team culture that everyone agrees to apply.

## WHEN INTERNATIONAL STAFFERS SHOW TOO MUCH RESPECT—OR TOO LITTLE

"In China, the boss is always right," says Steve Henning, reflecting on his years of managing in Beijing. "And even when the boss is very wrong, he is still right."

If, like Henning, you find yourself managing staff in a culture that is more hierarchical than your own, you may be surprised and uncomfortable to see how much importance is placed on what you say and how difficult it is to hear the opinions of those in positions below you. "When I would ask my staff members for their thoughts, advice, or opinions, they would sit quietly staring at their shoelaces," Henning remembers. "I later learned that this type of questioning suggested to them that I was trying to test them to see whether they knew what I wanted them to say. And since they didn't know, they felt it was safer to remain quiet."

For Henning this situation was initially perplexing. "How can I make good decisions if I don't know what my group really thinks about an issue?" he used to wonder. If you are managing a group that respects your authority so much that you are unable to get the input you need to make informed decisions, there are a few steps you can take without completely compromising the authority of your position. These strategies include:

- Ask your team to meet without you in order to brain-storm as a group—and then to report the group's ideas back to you. Removing "the boss" from the meeting re-moves their need to defer, allowing people to feel more comfortable sharing ideas.
- When you call a meeting, give clear instructions a few days beforehand about how you would like the meeting to work and what questions you plan to ask. Tell your team mem-bers explicitly that you will call on them for their input. In this way, they can show you respect by preparing and sharing their ideas. It also gives the team members time to organize their thoughts carefully and to check with one an-other before the meeting.
- If you are the boss, remember that your role is to chair the meeting. Don't expect people to jump in randomly without an invitation. Instead, invite people to speak up. Even if team members have prepared well and are ready to share their ideas, they may not volunteer unless you call on them individually. When you do so, you may be surprised to see how much they have to contribute.

On the other hand, you may find yourself in the same situation as Carlos Gomez, managing a group from a culture that is more egalitarian than your own. As Gomez explains, "I sometimes feel as if I have no idea what my staff is doing, because they rarely ask for feedback. For me, it has been a short step from feeling 'hands off' to feeling 'out of control.'"

Gomez began poring over management books recommended by his Dutch colleagues to learn their preferred leadership systems. He found that the management-by-objective system he had used in Mexico could easily be adapted to the egalitarian Dutch environment. His suggestions include the following:

- Introduce management by objectives, starting by speaking with each employee about the department's vision for the coming year and then asking them to propose their best personal annual objectives subject to negotiation and final agreement with you. In this way, you become a facilitator rather than a supervisor while still keeping a handle on what is being accomplished.
- Make sure the objectives are concrete and specific and consider linking them to bonuses or other rewards.
- Set objectives for a twelve-month period and check on progress periodically—perhaps once a month. If progress is satisfactory, you can give your subordinate more space for self-management; if progress lags, you can get more involved.

In addition, consider taking some simple symbolic steps to send appropriate signals about the leadership style you plan to employ. Dress as your team members dress—if they go without ties, do the same (except, of course, when a client visit or a presentation to the board of directors calls for a special "dress-up" protocol). Minimize the use of titles, addressing your team members by their first names—and encouraging them to do the same with you. And consider rotating the leadership role during staff meetings rather than retaining personal control of the discussion.

Actions like these will demonstrate your flexibility and allow your team members to feel comfortable working with you. After all, you are the one in the cultural minority, so it's up to you to adapt—if you are the boss.

*   *   *

After three years in the hierarchical, high-power-distance culture of Russia, Ulrich Jepsen had this to say:

> I've finally learned to lead well in this different environment, although it's taken a major shift in the way I look at my role as the boss. I can be friendly, as friendly as I would be in Denmark, but I have to maintain a greater distance with my staff and fulfill a type of paternalistic role that was new to me. Otherwise, my staff simply would not respect me or, worse, be embarrassed by me. And, as I quickly learned, without respect it is difficult to get anything done.

In today's global business environment it is not enough to be either an egalitarian leader or a hierarchical leader. You need to be both—to develop the flexibility to manage up and down the cultural scales. Often this means going back to square one. It means watching what makes local leaders successful. It means explaining your own style frequently. It may even mean learning to laugh at yourself when the right moment arises. But ultimately it means learning to lead in different ways in order to motivate and mobilize groups who *follow* in different ways from the folks back home.

# 5

## Big *D* or Little *d*

### Who Decides, and How?

A merger between a New York City financial firm and an organization in Germany proved to be one of the more tense cross-cultural deals I've worked on. Going into the merger, each group deeply admired the other, but misunderstandings quickly began breaking down the initial goodwill. A few months into the process, I interviewed the executive teams on each side to get their perspectives on how things were going. I began with Larry Nicoli, an intense, high-energy New Yorker with a lean figure and booming voice, who was number two in the company.

"Incredible! These Germans are incredibly hierarchical," Nicoli exclaimed. "I had lunch—just *lunch*—with one of the Munich-based analysts and later got my hand slapped by his boss's boss because he is several levels lower than me and I hadn't followed the proper protocol. Who cares what grade level he's at? Well, I learned one thing for certain—these Germans do!"

A few days later, I met with Matthias Wulf, the German HR executive who was leading the merger from the Munich side. He gave me quite an earful.

These Americans give you the impression they are so egalitarian with their open-door policies, first-name basis, and casual dress. Don't be fooled. They are much more hierarchical than we are! When the U.S. boss says "March left!" the Americans all click their heels and turn left—no question, no challenge. I've never seen anything like it. And if you are German, and you dare to challenge your American boss, as is so common in Germany, don't be surprised if you find yourself one step closer to unemployment. I know it's true—it happened to me!

If this had been my first experience working on a U.S.-German alliance, I might have been baffled by these seemingly contradictory complaints. Maybe I would have chalked them up to the organizational cultures of the groups, to the individual personalities involved—or to the universal human capacity for hypocrisy.

But having worked on similar deals in the past, I wasn't surprised by these comments. I was expecting them.

When I first moved from the United States to Europe, I was startled by the many remarks I heard from Germans and other northern Europeans about how hierarchical the American business culture is. We Americans believe deeply that we are an egalitarian people. But the more I listened to descriptions of American culture as viewed through a Germanic lens, the more I understood their point.

While Americans perceive German organizations as hierarchical because of the fixed nature of the hierarchical structure, the formal distance between the boss and subordinate, and the very formal titles used, Germans consider American companies hierarchical because of their approach to decision making. German culture places a higher value on building consensus as part of the decision-making process, while in the United States, decision making is largely invested in the individual.

## CONSENSUS IS A FOUR-LETTER WORD

I watched the best-selling author and popular American business speaker Patrick Lencioni giving a keynote address at an annual business conference in which he declared, "As far as I'm concerned, 'consensus' is a four-letter word! Consensus fails to satisfy anyone's desires, but it does so equally, and so it's accepted. It is through seeking consensus that we get mediocrity."[1]

Lencioni's disdain for group decision making reflects a common American sentiment—and this is what the Germans find incredible. Rejecting the need for group agreement, the American boss says to the group, "This is what we are going to do," and most members of the team fall in line, regardless of their own opinions. "United we stand, divided we fall," is a powerful American value, expressed in the belief that getting behind the decision as quickly as possible leads to efficiency, which in turn leads to success.

In this respect, American culture is one of a few outliers on the world map. Most cultures that fall as egalitarian on the Leading scale also believe in consensual decision making. The Swedes, for example, are both extremely egalitarian and one of the most consensual societies in the world. The Dutch also put a strong emphasis on both egalitarian leadership style and consensual decision making. By contrast, cultures that fall as hierarchical on the Leading scale, from Morocco to Korea, are also top-down decision-making cultures. In a large majority of countries, being egalitarian correlates with valuing consensus. The United States breaks the mold by combining an egalitarian ethos with a more top-down approach to decision making, in which one person—generally the person in charge—makes decisions quickly on behalf of the entire group. Therefore, the United States is more top-down than hierarchical. In comparison to a country like Germany or Sweden, the value is placed on one individual making a decision quickly and everyone else following. And this person tends to be the boss.

Conversely, there are a few cultures that break the mold in a different way. In countries like Germany, a consensual style of decision making, where more time is spent soliciting group feedback and coming to a group agreement, is combined with a hierarchical system. The fact that Germany and the United States are both exceptions to the global pattern—but in opposite directions—helps to explain the consternation among managers from these two cultures when they are thrown together in a decision-making situation.

The complications that can arise from differences in decision-making style don't stop there. Let's go back to the German-American merger talks. Given the trying circumstances, everyone involved was stressed and reacting reflexively. In hopes of creating an effective process for merging the two groups, the integration team, including both German and American managers, asked me to help.

My first meeting was with two German directors: Martina Müller, a small, expansive woman with her hair cut into a neat blond bob, and her more reserved but equally friendly boss, Matthias Wulf, who towered over Müller as they entered my office in Paris. When I asked them to describe the German managers' reactions to the last few months of integration efforts, they did not hold back.

Unsurprisingly, Müller and Wulf seemed particularly taken aback that the American CEO would make unilateral decisions, which the rest of the company would scurry to follow. By contrast, their previous German chairman had made all decisions through group agreement. "Even the agendas of the weekly management meetings are built by consensus," Müller explained. "The chairman distributes a proposed agenda days before the meeting, and everyone on the management board is asked to approve it or suggest changes—which would again be circulated for group approval before the actual meeting."

This difference in decision-making patterns had produced a deep sense of uneasiness among the Germans. "The problem," Müller explained, "is that we can't shake this feeling that the Americans are trying to trick us. We want to believe that they mean well, but we have quite consistently seen behavior that we feel is to the contrary."

Müller described how seemingly positive meetings with their American teammates would end with one of the Americans saying, "Great, we have made a decision." She continued, "And for us, when you say 'we will do this,' it is a commitment. A promise. You can't just simply change your mind casually tomorrow." The Germans were taken aback that the Americans could make decisions so quickly, without a lot of discussion and without involving all parties. In response, Müller said, "We would spend days on end working diligently on the implementation. And then one of the Americans would just change his mind, or bring in more data suggesting a different path. They casually change the decision every week, as if this was a normal part of teamwork."

"After much grief and frustration," Wulf added, "we have concluded that for Americans, a 'decision' is simply an agreement to continue discussions. And if you are American and you understand this, it is fine. But for a German, who sees a decision as a final commitment to march forward on a plan, this can cause a lot of problems."

Later, when I interviewed the American team, Larry Nicoli expressed deep frustration that the Germans seemed unable to adapt to new information: "It takes them weeks to make a decision, and, once it is made, they cling to it with their lives. But the world is dynamic. Things are changing. If decisions are not flexible, how can we beat the competition?"

As with other cultural characteristics, these differing styles of decision making have historical roots. American pioneers, many of whom had fled the formal hierarchical structures of their homelands, put heavy emphasis on speed and individualism. Being successful as the pioneers spread west across the American plains depended on arriving first and working hard, regarding mistakes as an inevitable and ultimately insignificant side effect of speed. As a corollary, Americans developed a dislike for too much discussion, which would just slow them down, preferring to make decisions quickly, often based on scanty information, whether by the leader or by voting.

Of course, today's American businesspeople are not looking for gold in California ditches or searching for arable farmland on empty plains, but this emphasis on rapid individual decision making, accompanied by the sense that decisions can always be changed, remains strong in the national culture.

By contrast, the preference for consensual decision making permeates many German companies, where power is generally vested not in one CEO but in a small group of senior managers who manage through group agreement. Larger companies have an *Aufsichtstrat*, or supervisory board, which appoints a *Vorstand*, or managerial board. The *Vorstand* has final decision-making responsibilities on company policies, and the chairman of the company therefore has considerably less individual power than in many other countries.

These differing styles of decision making have a dramatic impact on the timeline of a typical project. In a consensual culture, the timeline might look something like Figure 5.1.

**FIGURE 5.1.**

Discussion                                         Implementation
                                                   (no more discussion!)
_____|_____

**D**ecision

In a consensual culture, the decision making may take quite a long time, since everyone is consulted. But once the decision has been made, the implementation is quite rapid, since everyone has completely bought in and the decision is fixed and inflexible—a decision with a capital $D$, we might say. Thus, the moment of making the decision is taken quite seriously as the pivotal point in the process.

By contrast, in a top-down culture, the decision-making responsibility is invested in an individual. In this kind of culture, decisions tend to be made quickly, early in the process, by one person (likely the boss). But each decision is also flexible—a decision with a lowercase $d$. As more discussions occur, new information arises, or differing opinions surface, decisions may be easily revisited or altered. So plans are subject to continual revision—which means that implementation can take quite a long time (see Figure 5.2).

Either of these systems can work, as long as everyone understands and follows the rules of the game. But when the two

**FIGURE 5.2.**

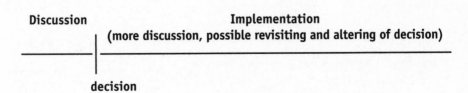

Discussion                    Implementation
                              (more discussion, possible revisiting and altering of decision)
_____|_____

        decision

systems collide, misunderstandings, inefficiency, and frustration can occur, as illustrated by the complaints that arose during the cross-cultural struggles of my American and German clients.

## CONSENSUAL OR TOP-DOWN: WHICH DO YOU PREFER?

As we've noted, both the United States and Germany are outliers on the Deciding scale. Although the United States falls toward the egalitarian end of the Leading scale, it appears toward the top-down side of the Deciding scale. Meanwhile, though Germany is characterized as a hierarchical culture on the Leading scale, it is marked by a consensus-oriented decision-making style. Aside from these two cultures, and one other we'll look at later in the chapter, most cultures have a similar position on the Leading and Deciding scales (see Figure 5.3).

In today's global business lexicon, the word "consensus" has a positive ring. It sounds inclusive and modern and is associated with other universally positive words like "empowerment." Thus, you may feel a sense of tribal pride if your country is positioned

### FIGURE 5.3. DECIDING

| Sweden | | Germany | | US | France | | India | Nigeria |
|---|---|---|---|---|---|---|---|---|
| Japan | Netherlands | | UK | | Brazil | Italy | Russia | China |

◄───────────────────────────────────────────────►

**Consensual**                                              **Top-down**

**Consensual**  Decisions are made in groups through unanimous agreement.

**Top-down**    Decisions are made by individuals (usually the boss).

on the consensus side of the scale and a prickle of tribal defensiveness if your culture is located on the top-down side.

However, when the time comes to make real decisions, it's clear that love for the process of consensus-building is anything but universal. I discovered this truth the first time I worked with a group of Swedes—members of a culture that is positioned on the far left of the Deciding scale.

Shortly after my first move to Europe, my new boss, Per Engman, introduced himself as a typical, consensus-building Swedish manager. He explained that this is the best way to assure that everyone was on board, and he hoped that I would be patient with this very Swedish process. I loved the sound of that. I was delighted with the idea of an inclusive boss, who listened carefully to his staff and weighed all of our views carefully before confirming a decision.

Our firm was a small consultancy with more work than we could handle, and my colleagues, mainly young, energetic Swedes, worked long hours to meet targets and keep our clients happy. Per was also hardworking and energetic, and I admired his relaxed way of dealing with the team—at least for my first two weeks on the job.

By then the e-mails had started mounting up in my in-box. One morning, this message arrived:

*Hey team*

*I thought we should meet for an annual face-to-face meeting on December 6th. We could focus the meeting on how to be more client-centric. What do you think?*

*Per*

I thought, "Well, I don't really have an opinion as to what the meeting is about, and I'm too busy to think much about it." I hit the delete button. But in the hours that followed, my Swedish colleagues began sending their responses:

> *Hi Per*
>
> *Great idea. Thanks for taking the initiative. Really looking forward to it. But we have focused so much on client-centricity lately. Wouldn't it be better to focus the meeting on how to more successfully market our services?*
>
> *Lasse*

> *Hi Per and everybody*
>
> *For this meeting I think it would be most effective to have presentations from each of the team members about their individual client strategies so that we can start to align our processes. If others don't agree then I would support Lasse's idea of focusing on marketing.*
>
> *Charlotte*

And one by one each of my colleagues sent a response with their opinions. Then there were more e-mails with responses to the responses. Occasionally, Per would inject an e-mail with a few comments. Slowly—ever so slowly, it seemed to me—they began to reach a group agreement. And then, after everyone but me had sent multiple replies, I received an individual e-mail.

*Hi Erin*

*Haven't heard from you, what do you think?*

*Per*

I really wanted to respond by saying, "I have absolutely no opinion. You are the boss—please make a decision so we can get back to work." Instead I reminded myself of how delighted I had felt when Per had told me that he favored a consensual decision-making style. So I simply replied that I supported whatever the group decided.

In the weeks to come, as many other topics got the same treatment, I realized that my gut instinct about myself had been wrong. In fact, consensual decision making was not at all the way I preferred to work. I also understood why Per had felt it necessary to explain his consensual approach to me so carefully before we started working together. He later described to me how it feels to be Swedish working with Americans, who are "too busy to work as good team members" and "always trying to impose a decision for decision's sake without soliciting the necessary feedback so that others feel bought in." That was me that Per was describing!

There are strong benefits to Per's inclusive consensual style. His team felt deeply listened to, and by the time the decisions were made, everyone was in agreement, so implementation was rapid. Yet from my own more top-down perspective, I would have gladly traded group agreement for the initial speed that goes with one person making a decision.

## THE JAPANESE RINGI SYSTEM: HIERARCHICAL BUT ULTRA-CONSENSUAL

As we have seen, the United States and Germany are two notable exceptions to the general pattern that egalitarian cultures tend to have consensus decision-making processes, while hierarchical cultures tend to practice top-down decision making. But the really remarkable exception is Japan, which although strongly hierarchical is one of the most consensual societies in the world. This seemingly paradoxical pattern grows from the fact that both hierarchical systems and consensual decision making are deeply rooted in Japanese culture.

The Japanese pharmaceutical company Astellas has large offices in the United Kingdom and the Netherlands. Jack Sheldon, who attended one of the seminars I conducted for Astellas, kept everyone laughing with stories about his mishaps while trying to work with Tokyo-based senior management.

"There was some problem with a new product, and a decision had to be made regarding whether to discontinue its development and testing," Sheldon explained.

A meeting was called at Tokyo headquarters at the end of the month and, as I am an expert on the matter and the decision would significantly impact my team's work, I was invited to attend. I felt very strongly that the testing should continue, and I worked diligently for three weeks to build up what I believed was a very convincing argument. All of the key players and decision-makers would be at the meeting in Tokyo, so I understood that what happened during those few hours would be critical. I prepared some slides for the meeting and requested time on the agenda to make my presentation.

When Sheldon arrived in the humidity and stifling August heat of Tokyo, he felt well prepared. "I love Tokyo, from the funny toilets that play music and squirt water at the press of a button to the multiple flavors of iced canned tea and coffee in the drink dispensers," he observes. "But I wasn't really prepared for the cultural differences I found in the meeting room."

I found myself in a large conference room with eight Japanese managers and two non-Japanese who were old hands at Astellas. The Japanese welcomed me graciously with bows and business cards and smiles. Everyone seemed to speak English well—a relief given that I know only six words in Japanese.

One of the Japanese managers gave an opening presentation, and during his speech he presented an argument followed by conclusions for why the testing should stop. I sensed that the others were in agreement with his comments. In fact, it seemed that the decision had already been finalized within the group. I presented my slides still feeling that my point of view would win out. But although people were very polite, it was clear that the Japanese managers were 100 percent aligned against continued testing. I gave all of my arguments and presented all of the facts, but the group wouldn't budge.

I felt a rush of frustration, which I managed with a lot of difficulty not to display. I had spent all this time preparing my argument and had flown across the world to meet with the group, yet discussing it with them had no effect at all.

Sheldon detailed this experience to our class with exasperation. As several of the participants were Japanese, I asked them to consider what might have happened and, if possible, to offer advice to Sheldon.

After a coffee break, Susumi Mori provided an explanation as a spokesperson for the Japanese participants. "In Japan, decisions tend to be made by group consensus rather than by the individual," Mori began. And he went on to explain what is called the *ringi* system of decision making. This is a management technique in which low-level managers discuss a new idea among themselves and come to a consensus before presenting it to managers one level higher.

Mori put it this way:

> During discussions, we pass around a proposal document, the *ringisho*, which usually begins at the mid-management level. When the proposal reaches each person, they read it, sometimes make changes or suggestions, and then put their stamp of approval on it. Once everyone has approved at one level, it passes on to the next.
>
> The next-higher-ranking managers then discuss the new idea themselves and arrive at their own consensus. If they agree, they pass the approval to the next level. This process continues until the idea reaches the highest management level and is or is not implemented. As you can see, the *ringi* system is hierarchical, bottom-up, and consensual all at the same time.
>
> By the time the *ringisho* document has made the rounds and received everyone's seal, all the people involved in the decision have had a chance to give input and are in agreement.

At Astellas, the *ringi* process is actually managed by a dedicated software program. The *ringi* system is often used by large, traditional Japanese corporations for big decisions. Even when the actual system is not used, decision making in Japanese organizations will often follow a similar process, with proposals beginning at a mid-level of management, collecting group agreement, and then moving up to the next hierarchical level for discussion. The end result is that the responsibility is spread out among many individuals rather than being concentrated with one or only a few.[2]

Before Japanese company members sign off on a proposal, consensus building starts with informal, face-to-face discussions. This process of informally making a proposal, getting input, and solidifying support is called *nemawashi*. Literally meaning "root-binding," *nemawashi* is a gardening term that refers to a process of preparing the roots of a plant or tree for transplanting, which protects them from damage. Similarly, *nemawashi* protects a Japanese organization from damage caused by disagreement or lack of commitment and follow-through.

With a longer, consensus-based decision-making process, implementation is quicker. Everyone is aware of the decision, most people agree with it, and careful planning has already taken place. When different groups or companies are involved, the long decision-making process fosters stronger and more trusting relationships. On the other hand, critics of the *ringi* system contend that it is time-consuming, allows individual managers to shirk accountability, and by the time the decision has been made, the race has likely been lost to those who moved more quickly. "Some Japanese companies have moved away from this system," one of Mori's colleagues explained, "but in Astellas we use a software product which manages the process."

"What I learned from the experience," Sheldon says, "is that, if I need to influence people at our Tokyo headquarters, I need to get involved very early in the discussions and do my 'root binding' well before the actual meeting. The more I can discuss the issues early in the decision-making process, the more impact I can make.

As the consensus builds support and momentum, it becomes very hard to go back on the group decision that has been reached."

The Japanese *ringi* system epitomizes a culture where decisions take a long time to be made, as everyone is invested in building a group consensus. But once the decision is made, it is generally fixed and the implementation may be very rapid, because each individual is on board. The result is a decision with a capital *D*.

## AVOIDING CULTURE CLASHES WHEN MAKING DECISIONS

Both consensual and top-down decision-making processes can be effective. But members of a global team often have expectations about decision making based on the norms of their own societies, which lead them to respond emotionally to what they see as ineffective behaviors of others on the team. Worse still, most of us are not even aware of the system our own culture uses to make decisions. We just follow the pattern without thinking about it—and this makes our defensive reactions to alternative approaches even more difficult to manage.

If you find yourself working with a team of people who employ a more consensual decision-making process than the one you're accustomed to, try applying the following strategies:

- Expect the decision-making process to take longer and to involve more meetings and correspondence.
- Do your best to demonstrate patience and commitment throughout the process . . . even when diverging opinions lead to seemingly interminable discussions and indecision.
- Check in with your counterparts regularly to show your commitment and be available to answer questions.

- Cultivate informal contacts within the team to help you monitor where the group is in the decision-making process. Otherwise, you may find that a consensus is forming without your awareness or participation.
- Resist the temptation to push for a quick decision. Instead, focus on the quality and completeness of the information gathered and the soundness of the reasoning process. Remember, once a decision is made, it will be difficult to try to change it.[3]

On the other hand, if you are working with a group of people who favor a more top-down approach to decision making, try using these techniques:

- Expect decisions to be made by the boss with less discussion and less soliciting of opinions than you are accustomed to. The decision may be made before, during, or after a meeting, depending on the organizational culture and the individual involved.
- Be ready to follow a decision even if your input was not solicited or was overruled. It's possible for a project to produce success even if the initial plan was not the best one that could have been devised.
- When you are in charge, solicit input and listen carefully to differing viewpoints, but strive to make decisions quickly. Otherwise you may find you are viewed as an indecisive or ineffective leader.
- When the group is divided about how to move forward and no obvious leader is present, suggest a vote. All members are expected to follow the decision supported by the majority, even if they disagree.

- Remain flexible throughout the process. Decisions are rarely set in stone; most can later be adjusted, revisited, or discussed again if necessary.

Finally, if you are working with a global team that includes members from both consensual and top-down cultures, you can avoid problems by explicitly discussing and agreeing upon a decision-making method during the early stages of your collaboration. Define whether the decision will be made by vote or by the boss after a team discussion. Determine whether 100 percent agreement is needed, whether a deadline for making the decision is necessary, and how much flexibility there will be for changing a decision after the deadline. Later, when big decisions must be made, revisit the decision-making process to make sure it is generally understood and accepted.

We used this approach to get the American/German merger talks back on track. It took time to build a shared awareness among the entire group about the differences in interpretations, habits, and perceptions between the American and German decision-making systems. Everyone was encouraged not to take themselves or their own style too seriously. This enabled the team members to talk openly about the problems and resolve them without acrimony.

In subsequent meetings, an American manager might be heard to say, "Great! Decision made!" only to pause and clarify: "Decision with a small *d*, that is! We still need to run this by our colleagues at home, so don't start work on it just yet!" And a German manager might conclude a discussion by asking, "So, have we agreed on a decision? And does it have a small *d* or a big *D*?"

The more both sides of the culture divide talked about it, the more natural it became for them to adjust to one another—and the more they enjoyed working together. As with so many challenges related to cross-cultural collaboration, awareness and open communication go a long way toward defusing conflict.

# 6

## The Head or the Heart

Two Types of Trust and How They Grow

Gerdau S.A., a household name throughout Brazil, is the four-teenth-largest steelmaker in the world, with operations in fourteen countries, including the United States and India. It was founded by Joo Gerdau, a German immigrant who moved to southern Brazil in 1869, and bought a nail factory in Puerto Alegre in 1901. He passed the business on to his son, Hugo Gerdau, who in turn passed it on to his son-in-law, Curt Johannpeter, in 1946.

Recently, working with a group of Gerdau executives, I heard firsthand the interesting backstory of one of Gerdau's recent acqui-sitions from Marina Morez, who headed up the discussions for the Brazilian Gerdau team, and from her American counterpart Jim Powly. The acquisition was a success, but the path there was full of interesting twists and turns.

"The meetings started well," said Morez, an exuberant woman in an elegant beige pants suit. "We traveled to Jacksonville, Mississippi, and Jim's team gave us a very friendly welcome. We got right down to business that morning." During three days of intense and sometimes difficult negotiations, the group proceeded steadily through the agenda, ordering in sandwiches for lunches and taking only short pauses throughout the day. At around seven each night, the exhausted group split up, the Americans heading home and the Brazilians retiring to their hotels.

At the end of the two days, the American team felt great about all they had accomplished. The discussions, they believed, were efficient and productive. The short lunches and tight scheduling signified respect for the time the Brazilians invested in preparing for the negotiations and traveling to an out-of-the-way location. The Brazilians, on the other hand, were less upbeat and felt the meetings had not gone as well as hoped. "Despite having spent two days together, we didn't know whether we could trust them," explained Morez. "They were certainly organized and efficient. But we didn't have a sense as to who they were beyond that. We didn't trust the Americans to deliver on their promises, and we wondered if they would make good partners."

Powly, who seemed to tower over the rest of us even when seated, continued the story. "Next, I brought the American team to Brazil to continue the discussions." Although the days were packed with meetings, the meals were long—lunches were frequently well over an hour, and dinners stretched into the late evening. The Brazilians took this opportunity to share good food and conversation with their American colleagues. "But we were uncomfortable," Powly remembers:

> As the first lunch stretched on, we started looking at our watches and shifting around in our chairs. We were worried about how we were possibly going to complete what we needed to accomplish. We wondered in the middle of these socializing marathons if the Brazilians were really taking these negotiations seriously.

What the Americans didn't understand was that these lunches and dinners symbolized something critical for the Brazilians. "For us, this type of lunch is supposed to send a clear message," Morez explained. "Dear colleagues, who have come such a long distance to work with us, we would like to show you that we respect you— and even if nothing else happens during these two days besides getting to know each other at a deeper level and developing a personal connection and trust, we will have made very good use of our time together."

The sense of discomfort felt by these two groups begins to show how differently Americans and Brazilians develop a sense of trust for one another. Of course, trust is a critical element of business in every country in the world. Whether your home is a small village in the Malaysian mountains or a glass-walled apartment atop a London skyscraper, you can't be successful if your colleagues, customers, partners, and suppliers don't trust you. But as the Gerdau merger story suggests, the means by which trust is built among business associates differ dramatically from one culture to another.

Powly and Morez managed to complete their deal without ever discovering the source of their discomfort. Nestlé's Karl Morel, who found himself in a similarly challenging situation, required more explicit advice to improve his effectiveness when negotiating a joint venture in China.

An acquisitions expert from the German-speaking region of Switzerland, Morel led a negotiation team for multinational food giant Nestlé. The team traveled to Shanghai to explore a potential joint venture with a company specializing in packaged Chinese delicacies.

The initial meetings with eight Chinese executives proved to be a baffling experience for Morel. While he and his colleagues tried to be friendly and transparent, providing all the business details the Chinese asked for, the Chinese seemed closed and secretive. "They were impenetrable. They were tough as nails and unwilling to budge on any of their demands. That first week was one uphill battle after another," Morel recalls. Fortunately, after the first frustrating week, Morel and his colleagues met with a Chinese business consultant who pushed them to rethink their approach:

> When we contacted the Chinese consultant, we were desperate. We had spent months identifying the best possible group to partner with, flown 5,000 miles to Shanghai, and invested a full week in meetings, but we didn't seem to be getting anywhere.
>
> The consultant told us that our approach was wrong, that we were going too fast. We argued that we had been very detailed, open, and patient. But the consultant was clear about what we were doing wrong. He told us that we were not going to get what we wanted from the Chinese executives unless we developed *guanxi* with them.

*Guanxi?* Morel and his team had never heard the word. The consultant explained:

> What I mean is that you should take the time, energy, and effort to build a personal connection with them. Build trust as a friend from the heart. Forget the deal for a while. Go out. Enjoy some meals. Share some drinks. Relax. Build an emotional connection. Open up personally. Make a friend. A real one, the kind with whom you are willing to let your guard down.

Morel and his colleagues took the consultant's advice. They invited their Chinese counterparts for a dinner one evening over a weekend, bringing together people from several hierarchical levels of both organizations. The evening was a great success. "We went to a restaurant on a barge in the river," Morel remembers:

> There was live guitar music and huge amounts of food from the Tianjin area of China, where the owner of the other company came from. It was an excellent dinner, during which we had time to socialize. We focused on having fun, and we stopped talking about business. The group toasted each other several times in a sign of mutual respect and emphasized how glad we all were to begin a long-term relationship. We laughed a lot—and a few of us drank a lot.
>
> We restarted the meetings the following Monday, and the Chinese willingness to cooperate had changed considerably. They were now very enthusiastic and open, and we began to work well as a team. We were able to make very good progress during our second week in China.

Both the Swiss and the Chinese recognize the importance of trust in business relationships—but they make very different unconscious assumptions about how trust is created.

## TRUST FROM THE HEAD, TRUST FROM THE HEART

Make a quick mental list of five or six people you trust—people from different areas of your life. The list may include personal connections like your mother or your spouse, but may also include a business partner, a client, or a supplier. Then consider for a moment how the trust you feel for each person was built. What events led you to trust them?

You might notice that the type of trust you feel for one person is very different from the type of trust you feel for another. The differences can be complex, but one simple distinction is between two forms of trust: *cognitive trust* and *affective trust*.

Cognitive trust is based on the confidence you feel in another person's accomplishments, skills, and reliability. This is trust that comes from the head. It is often built through business interactions: We work together, you do your work well, and you demonstrate through the work that you are reliable, pleasant, consistent, intelligent, and transparent. Result: I trust you.

Affective trust, on the other hand, arises from feelings of emotional closeness, empathy, or friendship. This type of trust comes from the heart. We laugh together, relax together, and see each other at a personal level, so that I feel affection or empathy for you and sense that you feel the same for me. Result: I trust you.

Throughout the world, friendships and personal relationships are built on affective trust. If you were to consider why you trust your mother or your spouse, you would likely use descriptive explanations linked to affective trust. But the source of trust in business relationships is a little more complicated.

Roy Chua, a professor at Harvard Business School, surveyed Chinese and American executives from a wide range of industries, asking them to list up to twenty-four important members of their professional networks, from both inside and outside their own workplaces. Then participants were asked to indicate the extent to which they felt comfortable going to each of these contacts to share their personal problems and difficulties as well as their hopes and dreams. "These items showed an affective-based willingness to depend on and be vulnerable to the other person." Chua explains. Finally, participants were asked to indicate the extent to which the contact could be relied on to complete a task that he or she has agreed to do as well as to have the knowledge and competence needed to get tasks done. These items captured a more cognitive-based willingness to depend on the other person.[1]

The survey revealed marked differences between the American respondents and the Chinese. Chua found that Americans, in business, draw a sharp dividing line between cognitive trust and affective trust. "This finding makes sense given culture and history," Chua explains. The United States has "a long tradition of separating the practical and emotional. Mixing the two is perceived as unprofessional and risks conflict of interest."

Chinese managers, on the other hand, connect the two forms of trust. As Chua puts it, "Among Chinese executives, there is a stronger interplay between affective and cognitive trust. Unlike Americans, Chinese managers are quite likely to develop personal ties and affective bonds when there is also a business or financial tie." One consequence is that, for a Chinese manager working with Americans, the culturally based preference to separate cognitive trust and personal trust can indicate a lack of sincerity or loyalty.

During a research project I worked on with my longtime collaborator Elisabeth Shen, we interviewed Jing Ren, a thirty-five-year-old Chinese sales manager, who was taken aback to learn how little a personal relationship meant when working in the United States. "In China," Ren says, "if we have lunch together, we can build a relationship that leads to us working together. But here in Houston, it doesn't work like that."

Ren hadn't been looking to develop a friendship when he bumped into Jeb Bobko at the gym:

I was working out on the rowing machine when I asked him what time it was. We started talking, and I learned that he was preparing for an upcoming monthlong trip across China.

We had a great first connection, and he invited me to his house for dinner several times with his wife and children, and I invited him back. I got to know him and his family well. We developed a great relationship.

Just by chance, his organization was a potential client for us, and I have to say that initially I thought that was great luck. But when we started discussing how our organizations would work together, I was taken aback to find that Jeb wanted to look at every detail of the contract closely and negotiate the price as if I was a stranger. He was treating me as if we had no relationship at all.

In Ren's culture, personal trust fundamentally shifts the way the two parties conduct business. By contrast, American managers make a concerted effort to ensure that personal relationships do not cloud the way they approach business interactions—in fact, they often deliberately restrict affective closeness with people they depend on for economic resources, such as budgeting or financing.

After all, in countries like the United States or Switzerland, "business is business." In countries like China or Brazil, "business is personal."

## TASK-BASED VERSUS RELATIONSHIP-BASED CULTURES

Of course, China and Brazil are not the only cultures where affective and cognitive trust are mixed together in business relationships. On the Trusting scale, countries are rated from high task-based to high relationship-based (Figure 6.1). The further a

## FIGURE 6.1. **TRUSTING**

| US Denmark Germany | UK | Poland | France Italy | Mexico Brazil | Saudi Arabia |
|---|---|---|---|---|---|
| Netherlands Finland | | | Spain | Russia Thailand India | |
| Australia | | Austria | | Japan Turkey China Nigeria | |

← ——————————————————————————————————— →

**Task-based**                                    **Relationship-based**

...............................................................................................

| **Task-based** | Trust is built through business-related activities. Work relationships are built and dropped easily, based on the practicality of the situation. You do good work consistently, you are reliable, I enjoy working with you, I trust you. |
|---|---|
| **Relationship-based** | Trust is built through sharing meals, evening drinks, and visits at the coffee machine. Work relationships build up slowly over the long term. I've seen who you are at a deep level, I've shared personal time with you, I know others well who trust you, I trust you. |

culture falls toward the task-based end of the scale, the more people from that culture tend to separate affective and cognitive trust, and to rely mainly on cognitive trust for work relationships. The further a culture falls toward the relationship-based end of the scale, the more cognitive and affective trust are woven together in business.

As you look at the Trusting scale you see the United States positioned far to the left while all BRIC countries (Brazil, Russia, India, and China) fall far to the right. When it comes to building trust, the center of gravity in the global business world has fundamentally shifted over the past fifteen years. Previously, managers working in global business may have felt themselves pulled toward working in a more American manner, because the United States dominated most world markets. Building trust in a task-based fashion was therefore one of the keys to international success. But in today's business environment, the BRIC cultures are rising and expanding their reach. At the same time, countries in the southern hemisphere such as Indonesia and Saudi Arabia are growing in global weight. All of these countries lie markedly toward the relationship-based end of the Trusting scale. Today if you are a manager aiming for success at an international level and your work brings you to the BRIC cultures or really anywhere in the southern hemisphere, you must learn how to build relationship-based trust with your clients and colleagues in order to be successful.

On the other hand, for those who work frequently in North America, you may be skeptical about the accuracy of the United States on the left-hand side of the Trusting scale. Are Americans really so task-based? What about the client breakfasts, the golf outings, and the team-building activities and icebreaker exercises featured at so many American-style training programs or conferences? Don't these suggest that Americans are just as relationship-based as the Brazilians or the Chinese?

Not really. Think back to those icebreaker activities—those two-to-three-minute exchanges designed to "build a relationship" between complete strangers. What happens when the exercise is completed? Once the relationship is built, the participants check it off the list and get down to business—and at the end of the program, the relationships that were so quickly built are usually just as quickly dropped.

What's true in the training or conference center is true outside of it. In task-based societies like the United States, the United Kingdom, and Australia, relationships are defined by functionality and practicality. It is relatively easy to move in and out of networks, and if a business relationship proves to be unsatisfactory to either party, it's a simple matter to close the door on that relationship and move into another.

By contrast, icebreaker exercises in relationship-based societies are rare. Relationships are built up slowly, founded not just

on professional credibility but also on deeper emotional connections—and after the relationship is built, it is not dropped easily.

As an example, consider what happens when the boss fires
someone on your team. Will you continue your relationship with
the person who has been fired even though he is no longer part of
your company? Responses to this question vary dramatically from
one culture to another.

A Spanish executive working in an American firm told me:

> I couldn't believe the way my American colleagues reacted when
> one of our team members lost his job. That guy was our friend
> one day and out of our lives the next. I asked my teammates—all
> of whom I respect deeply—"When are we going to have a party
> for him, meet him for drinks, tell him he is on our minds?" They
> looked at me as if I was a little crazy. They seemed to feel, since
> he was underperforming, we could just push him off the boat
> and pretend we never cared about him. For a Spaniard, this is
> not an easy thing to accept.

If a Spanish manager finds the American attitude strange,
a Chinese manager is likely to find it unthinkable. John Trott, a
Canadian working in pharmaceuticals and living in Shanghai, explains, "In China, business relationships *are* personal relationships.
The loyalty is to the individual and not to the company. If someone
leaves the company, the personal relationship would be much stronger than the severance between that person and the organization."

The ramifications for someone managing a Chinese team are
immediately apparent. If you fire a salesperson, the client who had
a relationship with him may also choose to leave. Likewise, if you
fire a sales manager who has strong affective trust with his team
members, the best are likely to follow him to his new company.

This difference between the way Americans react to a firing and the way those from relationship-based cultures react underscores the reality that Americans are, in fact, highly task-based—no matter how many "relationship building" exercises they may perform at conferences or seminars.

## PEACH VS. COCONUT: FRIENDLY DOES NOT EQUAL RELATIONSHIP-BASED

Just as it is easy to misinterpret the reason for an icebreaker activity, it's easy to mistake certain social customs of Americans that might suggest strong personal connections where none are intended. For example, Americans are more likely than those from many cultures to smile at strangers and to engage in personal discussions with people they hardly know. Others may interpret this "friendliness" as an offer of friendship. Later, when the Americans don't follow through on their unintended offer, those other cultures often accuse them of being "fake" or "hypocritical."

Igor Agapova, a Russian colleague of mine, tells this story about his first trip to the United States:

> I sat down next to a stranger on the airplane for a nine-hour flight to New York. This American began asking me very personal questions: did I have any children, was it my first trip to the U.S., what was I leaving behind in Russia? And he began to also share very personal information about himself. He showed me pictures of his children, told me he was a bass player, and talked about how difficult his frequent traveling was for his wife, who was with his newborn child right now in Florida.

In response, Agapova started to do something that was unnatural for him and unusual in Russian culture—he shared his personal story quite openly with this friendly stranger, thinking they had built an unusually deep friendship in a short period of time. The sequel was quite disappointing:

> I thought that after this type of connection, we would be friends for a very long time. When the airplane landed, imagine my surprise when, as I reached for a piece of paper in order to write down my phone number, my new friend stood up and with a friendly wave of his hand said, "Nice to meet you! Have a great trip!" And that was it. I never saw him again. I felt he had purposely tricked me into opening up when he had no intention of following through on the relationship he had instigated.

Kurt Lewin[2] was one of the first social scientists to explain individual personality as being partially formed by the cultural system in which a person was raised. Authors Fons Trompenaars and Charles Hampden-Turner later expanded on Lewin's model to explain how different cultures have different layers of information that they divulge publicly or reserve for private relationships.[3] These models are frequently referred to as the peach and coconut models of personal interaction.

In peach cultures like the United States or Brazil, to name a couple, people tend to be friendly ("soft") with others they have just met. They smile frequently at strangers, move quickly to first-name usage, share information about themselves, and ask personal questions of those they hardly know. But after a little friendly interaction with a peach person, you may suddenly get to the hard shell of the pit where the peach protects his real self. In these cultures, friendliness does not equal friendship.

When conducting a workshop in Brazil, one of the German participants who had been living in Rio de Janeiro for a year explained,

> People are so friendly here. It is unbelievable. You might be buying groceries or simply crossing the street. People ask you questions, speak about their families, and they are constantly inviting you over for a cup of coffee or suggesting that they'll see you tomorrow on the beach. At the beginning I felt so happy to receive so many invitations of friendship. But it didn't take long for me to realize that all those people who invite me over for coffee keep forgetting to tell me where they live and those constant suggestions that we'll meet on the beach the next day simply never materialize. Because the beach is, of course, many miles long.

In Minnesota, where I was raised, we learn at a very young age to smile generously at people we've just met. That's one characteristic of a peach culture. A Frenchwoman who visited with my family was taken aback by Minnesota's "peachiness." "The waiters here are constantly smiling and asking me how my day is going! They don't even know me. It makes me feel uncomfortable and suspicious. What do they want from me? I respond by holding tightly on to my purse."

On the other hand, coming from a peach culture as I do, I was equally taken aback when I came to live in Europe. My friendly smiles and personal comments were greeted with such cold formality by the Polish, French, German, or Russian colleagues I was just beginning to know. I took their stony expressions as signs of arrogance, perhaps even hostility.

In coconut cultures such as these, people are more closed (like the tough shell of a coconut) with those they don't have friendships with. They rarely smile at strangers, ask casual acquaintances personal questions, or offer personal information to those they don't know intimately. It takes a while to get through the initial hard shell, but as you do, people will become gradually warmer and friendlier. While relationships are built up slowly, they tend to last longer.

When you travel to a coconut culture, the receptionist at the company you are visiting will not ask, "What did you do this weekend?" and the hairdresser who is cutting your hair for the first time will not remark, "An American married to a Frenchman? How did you meet your husband?" If you are a peach person traveling in a coconut culture, be aware of the Russian saying "If we pass a stranger on the street who is smiling, we know with certainty that that person is crazy . . . or else American." If you enter a room in Moscow (or Belgrade, Prague, or even Munich or Stockholm) and find a group of solemn-looking managers who make no effort to chat, do not take this as a sign that the culture does not value relationship building. On the contrary, it is through building a warm personal connection over time that your coconut-culture counterparts will become trusting, loyal partners.

The point, of course, is that different cultures have different social cues that mark appropriate behavior with strangers as opposed to cues that indicate a real friendship is developing. People from both task-based cultures and relationship-based cultures may be affable with strangers, but this characteristic does not in itself indicate either friendship or relationship orientation.

## STRATEGIES FOR BUILDING TRUST ACROSS CULTURAL DIVIDES

As a general rule of thumb, investing extra time developing a relationship-based approach will pay dividends when working with people from around the world. This is true even if you both come from task-based cultures, such as the United States and Germany. Once an affective relationship is established, the forgiveness for any cultural missteps you make comes a lot easier. So when you work internationally, no matter who you are working with, investing more time in building affective trust is a good idea. But knowing exactly how to build affective trust may not always be so obvious.

One productive way to start putting trust deposits in the bank is by building on common interests. Wolfgang Schwartz, from Austria, used this simple way of connecting with people to great success during two decades of work in Russia. "When I retired and left Moscow," he said, "I was replaced by a younger Austrian colleague, Peter Geginat, who had an extraordinary track record in Austria but knew nothing about how people outside of Austria work. His task-based approach was effective for Austria, but not at all suited for Russia."

Geginat worked diligently for months to close an attractive deal with a potential client. He invested countless hours in making his presentation outstanding, his brochures polished, and his offer generous and transparent. Yet the client dragged his feet, and, six months into the process, his interest seemed to be dwindling. At this point, the young Geginat called Schwartz up and asked for advice, given the latter's success during all those years in Russia.

Schwartz came to Moscow and met directly with the client:

The first thing I noticed when I saw him was that he was about my age—we both have white hair. So I spoke of my family, and we spent the first half hour talking about our grandchildren. Then I noticed he had a model of a fighter plane on his desk. I also flew planes in the military, and I saw this as an incredible opportunity. We spent the next hour talking about the differences between various military planes.

At this point, the Russian client signaled that he had to leave. But he invited me to go with him to the ballet that evening. Now, in truth, I dislike the ballet. But I'm not stupid. When an opportunity this good comes along, I jump on it. The evening went beautifully and ended in a drink with the client and his wife.

At 10:00 a.m. the next day, Schwartz met again with the client, who said, "I've looked through your proposal, I understand your situation, and I agree with your terms. I have to get someone else to sign the contract, but if you would like to take the plane back to Austria today I will fax you the signed contract this afternoon." When Schwartz arrived at his office in Austria the next Monday morning, the €2 million down payment was already in his account. Schwartz was able to accomplish more in twenty-four hours with a relationship-based approach than his task-based colleague was able to accomplish in six months.

You might protest that Schwartz was remarkably lucky. Just by chance, he happened to have several things in common with his Russian client, from grandchildren to fighter planes, and in fact, Schwartz did end his account by exclaiming, "It was my white hair that saved me!" But Schwartz found these similarities because he was looking for them.

If you are working with someone from a relationship-based culture and opportunities for a personal connection don't jump out at you, it is worth the investment to look a little harder—as Italian Alberto Gaiani found when he worked with a team of young software engineers based in Mumbai, India.

"I couldn't imagine what we could possibly have in common," Gaiani told me. "I was well aware from past experiences that, in order to manage a team of Indians effectively, it is absolutely critical to develop a good relationship with them." But Gaiani had two challenges. The bigger challenge was the fact that he couldn't travel because of budget cuts. The smaller was his personal background, so strikingly different from that of his Indian team members. As Gaiani explained,

> I am forty-six years old with four children. My life is homework and diapers and weekend trips to grandma's house. But one thing I do love is music. I listen to music in the car, in the shower, while I'm working. Classical, rock, you name it. So then it occurred to me, why not use Indian pop music to make a connection?
>
> I Googled "Indian pop music what's hot." Then I spent two hours listening to the top songs that came up on YouTube and getting a feel for the rhythms and beats. For the song I liked the best, I sent my Indian staff a link. "Do you know this song?" I asked them. "Do you love it like I do?" They responded with a resounding "NO, we don't like that song—are you kidding?" "This is my twelve-year-old sister's favorite song! You can do better than that!" one of them told me. And then they sent me links to the songs they liked. I created a great dialogue with them over something that was very interesting to all of us personally.

The time it took for Gaiani to investigate which songs were hot in Mumbai paid off in myriad intangible ways. As he says, "In the past I have often had the experience with Indian employees such that, if you don't develop a good personal relationship with them, they will tell you everything is okay even if the entire project has gone up in flames. Once the relationship is built, loyalty and openness comes with it."

What makes Gaiani's example particularly powerful is that he managed to do all this relationship building without ever meeting with his staff face-to-face. This, of course, is the reality that many of us face today. We work with people in countries on the opposite side of the planet, knowing very little about their cultural context. This makes relationship building more difficult, but no less important.

## SHOWING YOUR TRUE SELF: THE RELATIONSHIP IS THE CONTRACT

Picture this situation: You are on a business trip, and after a full day of formal meetings, a potential client has invited you out to dinner. As drinks are served and delicious smells roll out of the kitchen, how do you feel?

*Careful to maintain your professional composure. You want to be certain that you don't drink too much or let down your guard and make a bad impression. You are friendly, attentive, and trying to connect with the client, but careful to put your best foot forward at all times.*

Or

*Ready to let go. You have been focused on business all day long— now is the time to have some fun, develop friendships, show who you are outside of a business setting, and get to know others beyond their work personas. You share drinks, open up, and relax without concern.*

As my roots are in a task-based culture and I worked for the first several years of my career in the United States, my assumption was that the first scenario—caution—is the most proper answer. My strong belief was that when among people who could have any impact on my business success—not just clients but colleagues and other associates—I should always show the best "me" possible. The ditzy, forgetful "me" who loses her keys and forgets her purse at restaurants—not to mention the fun-loving, noisy "me" who often talks more than she listens and has lots of accidental-bad-mother stories to report—should be reserved for family and friends.

But time and experience have taught me that the second scenario, show your nonprofessional self, is often the better approach when working with relationship-based cultures. I initially learned this lesson when working with Repsol, the Spanish oil giant. Ricardo Bartolome, who worked on a global team in the company's Texas office, gave me this valuable insight:

> One of the aspects I find so difficult about working with Americans is that, although they are very friendly, sometimes surprisingly so, they don't show you who they really are in a business relationship. They are so politically correct. They don't dare complain or show negative emotion.
>
> In Spanish culture, we put a strong value on the importance of being *authentico*, and we perceive Americans as not authentic. You can work with an American supplier for years and hear all about his family, his weekends, his children, but everything is wrapped up in a package of positivity that we Europeans feel is impenetrable.
>
> My colleagues call Americans superficial and fake, but I don't see it that way. I think they are just very, very careful to not show business counterparts who they really are. In either case, it makes it hard for us to trust them.

Bartolome's comments got me thinking about the downside of maintaining a "professional" demeanor in all my interactions with business acquaintances. Another mind-shifter for me was a conversation with Ted Krooner, an American whose work brought him frequently to Latin America. Krooner complained:

> I just get so exhausted on those trips to Mexico. After a long day of meetings, we go out to a restaurant and then out for more drinks. I can hang on for an hour, or an hour and a half. But the evenings drag on and on. They are drinking and laughing, really having a great time . . . but I feel like my head is about to hit the table. I just can't concentrate any longer.

I sympathized with Krooner, having felt the same way during my own evenings with business associates in Latin America. But as I reflected on his words, I began to recognize in Krooner what I hadn't really understood about myself. Krooner felt exhausted after a night of partying because "he couldn't concentrate any longer." But his relationship-based colleagues had left concentration behind when they entered the restaurant.

The best strategy in this situation is to join the crowd. When working in a relationship-based culture such as Mexico, the moment you switch from boardroom to restaurant or bar is the moment you need to begin acting as if you are out on the town with your best friends. Don't worry about saying or doing the wrong thing. Be yourself—your personal self, not your business self. Dare to show that you have nothing to hide, and the trust—and likely the business—will follow.

Of course, a focus on keeping a professional persona isn't the only reason task-based people find it hard to adjust to relationship-based cultures. Investing hours in building affective trust can seem time-consuming and wasteful. In the words of a Danish oil executive who had recently moved to Lagos, Nigeria, "Who has time? Of course we all know that relationship building is key in Nigeria, but I'm very busy. If I spend the time and energy necessary to build affective trust with my Nigerian suppliers, I simply won't have time to get my job done."

It's an understandable complaint—and it raises an obvious question: Why do people in cultures like Nigeria, India, or Argentina invest so much time in relationship building? Is it simply that they are inefficient or prefer socializing to working?

There is, in fact, a very clear, practical benefit to investing in affective relationship building—especially when working in emerging markets. This brings us back to the business value of trust.

Suppose you are the Danish owner of a business that designs women's purses. You sell two hundred purses wholesale to a shop that has just opened on the other side of Copenhagen. You give the retailer the purses, and he promises to pay you next week. How do you know you are going to get your money?

The answer, of course, is that the shop owner signed a contract promising to pay you. If he doesn't pay, you can take him to court. Having a signed agreement in a culture with a consistently reliable legal system makes it possible to do business easily with people you don't trust or even know.

Now imagine the same situation—only this time you are Nigerian and designing women's purses in Lagos. The legal system in Nigeria is less reliable than the one found in countries such as Denmark, the United Kingdom, and the United States. You can sign a contract, but there is no way of enforcing it if the payment doesn't come through.

The only way you feel assured that you'll be paid in countries like Nigeria is the trust you have in the other person. Perhaps he has done business with your brother for years and your brother vouches for him; perhaps you've worked with his cousins or close friends on other projects; or perhaps you've had time to get to know him personally and you've concluded that he is trustworthy. You believe you can do business with the shopkeeper because your relationship with him (direct or indirect) provides a safety net that replaces the role of the legal system in more developed countries.

For this reason, investing time in establishing trust will often *save* time (and many other resources) in the long run. And a similar way of thinking continues to exist in relationship-based cultures that are also blessed with solidly reliable legal structures, such as Japan and France.

So if you find yourself wondering in exasperation, "Why do I have to spend so much time dining and socializing with potential clients? Why can't we just get down to business and sign a contract?" remember—in many cultures, the relationship *is* your contract. You can't have one without the other.

## CONSIDER MEALS CAREFULLY: LUNCH MAY BE YOUR TICKET

How you organize and conduct your lunches and dinners when collaborating with people from other cultures can communicate volumes—often unintentionally, as I found out from an e-mail I received from Guillermo Nuñez, an Argentine executive with a global wine distributor:

> Last year, I had a strange experience when some of my colleagues and I visited one of our bulk wine customers in Norway. I was

giving a presentation to these Norwegians about our Argentinean office, and explaining the challenges that we had crossing the fjords with our container boats. Up until that point, I thought that the presentation was going well.

Then one of the Norwegians interrupted me, in a very polite way, just to inform me that they had ordered some sandwiches and drinks to have during the meeting. I was really surprised. This signaled to me that they were not interested in what I was saying. Never in my thirty years of working across Latin America had something like this happened to me.

I was confused about what to do. Should I continue to talk although they clearly were interested in eating their sandwiches? I did finish my presentation, but I felt completely stupid speaking while they were eating their lunch.

After the meeting, I spoke to my Norwegian-based colleague about what I'd felt had been a disastrous hour. He told me that I had misunderstood and that the situation was very normal. He explained that Norwegians often do this just to optimize time. He said it was a sign of respect for our time, which they would like to invest wisely.

Nuñez actually assumed that his colleague from Norway was simply trying to spare his feelings. Not until he attended a program I conducted and spoke about cross-cultural trust building did he discover that his lunchtime "disaster" was really just a case of crossed signals.

The good news is that strategies for improving trust are quite simple, often requiring only a few minor adjustments in your expectations and behaviors.

The first strategy is easy. If you are from a task-based society and are hosting people from a more relationship-based society, put more time and effort into organizing meals to be shared. During these meals, spend time getting to know your collaborators personally rather than discussing business. And if you are visiting a relationship-based culture, don't mistake a long lunch for a waste of time. If you use this time to develop a personal connection and a little affective trust, it may end up being the most important part of the business trip.

For those from relationship-based societies who are hosting task-based guests, don't throw out the socializing altogether. Go ahead and organize a one-hour lunch, which they will most certainly appreciate. But if the meal is likely to stretch on to ninety minutes or longer, explain this in advance. And feel free to invite your task-based colleagues out in the evening—but if one of them chooses to go back to the hotel to get some rest or catch up on e-mails, don't take offense. This is a normal and appropriate response in a task-based culture.

Sharing meals is a meaningful tool for trust building in nearly all cultures. But in some cultures, sharing drinks—particularly alcoholic drinks—is equally important.

I once conducted a training program for a German couple moving to Japan, assisted by Hiroki, a wise and entertaining Japanese culture specialist. The German asked Hiroki how to get his Japanese colleagues to tell him what was really going on: "They are so formal and quiet. I worry if I am not able to build the necessary trust, I won't get the information I need from them."

Hiroki thought quietly for a moment and then responded with only a small trace of humor in his eyes: "Best strategy is to drink with them."

"To drink?" the German client questioned.

"Yes, drink until you fall down."

When Hiroki said this, I thought back to my first-ever ride in the Tokyo metro, when I saw several groups of Japanese businessmen stumbling through the station as they traveled home after a long evening of well-lubricated socializing. I now realized they were following Hiroki's advice—quite literally.

If you look at Japan on the Trusting scale, you will see that it is a relationship-based culture, though not as far to the right as China or India. During the day, the Japanese generally take a task-based approach—but the relationship building that happens in the evening can be critical to business success.

In Japanese culture, where group harmony and avoiding open conflict are overriding goals, drinking provides an opportunity to let down your hair and express your real thoughts. Drinking is a great platform for sharing your true inner feelings (what are called *honne* rather than *tatemae* feelings) as well as for recognizing where bad feelings or conflict might be brewing and to strive to address them before they turn into problems. Under no circumstances should the discussions of the night before be mentioned the next day. Drinking alcohol is therefore an important Japanese bonding ritual not only with clients, but also within one's own team.

Many Japanese use drinking to forge connections, as captured by the bilingual expression *nomunication*, stemming from the Japanese verb *nomu* ("to drink"). Japanese salespeople frequently woo their clients over drinks, knowing that although explicit deal making is never done during this type of socializing, a deal is rarely won without it. Of course, drinking to build trust is not just a Japanese custom. Across East Asia, whether you are working in China, Thailand, or Korea, doing a substantial amount of drinking with customers and collaborators is a common step in the trust-building process.

Many people from task-based cultures don't get it. "Why would I risk making a fool of myself in front of the very people I need to impress?" they wonder. But that is exactly the point. When you share a round of drinks with a business partner, you show that person you have nothing to hide. And when they "drink until they fall down" with you, they show you that they are willing to let their guard down completely. "Don't worry about looking stupid," Hiroki reassured our German manager, who had begun wringing his hands nervously. "The more you are willing to remove social barriers in the evening, the more they will see you as trustworthy."

Alcohol is not the only way to build a business relationship. If you don't drink, you can certainly find other ways to partake in the fun; in Japan, a round of karaoke or a trip to the spa can do wonders. And in Arab cultures, where alcohol is avoided, you can forget beer and relax instead over a cup of tea.

## CHOOSE YOUR COMMUNICATION MEDIUM:
## PHONE, E-MAIL, OR WASTA

Of course, in today's global business world, not all relationships provide the opportunity for face-to-face sharing over a meal or a drink. A lot of trust building must take place long-distance. Most of us send an e-mail or pick up the telephone without giving culture much thought. However, putting a little effort into the choice can help tremendously when you need to build trust with your globally-dispersed colleagues.

If you are working with people from a task-based society, go ahead and choose the medium that is the most efficient, if that is your preference. E-mail, telephone, face-to-face meetings—all are acceptable, so long as the message is communicated clearly and succinctly.

But when starting to work with those from a relationship-based society, begin by choosing a communication medium that is as relationship-based as possible. Instead of sending an e-mail, make the extra effort to pick up the phone. Better still, if you have the budget as well as the time, take the trip. And don't pack your day with task-based meetings and expect to escape to your hotel in the evening. Organize your time in order to communicate as much as possible in informal settings. Once you have built a good trusting relationship, you can move to a more task-based medium like e-mail.

E-mail can be particularly problematic when you are trying to make a connection with a person you don't know. In task-based cultures, it is quite common to e-mail people you've never met. However, in relationship-based cultures, people often don't respond to e-mails from someone with whom they have no prior relationship.

One strategy, if you need to contact someone you don't know, is to use what in Arabic is called *wasta*, which translates loosely to mean something like "connections that create preference," "relationships that give you influence," or "who you know." Dana Al-Hussein, a Jordanian manager working for L'Oréal, explains the concept:

> A good personal relationship is the single most important factor when doing business with people from the Arab world. If you don't have a relationship, don't resort to e-mailing strangers out of the blue. Use your network to find a *wasta*—someone who has a relationship with the person you need to contact, and ask that person to make a quick call introducing you personally. A friend of a friend can work wonders in establishing a first step to a personal connection.

If you take this approach, you are likely to find your e-mails answered rapidly.

Furthermore, whether using phone, e-mail, or working face-to-face, think carefully about the amount of time you will devote to social talk before getting down to business.

In just about every culture, when you make a phone call, you are likely to start with a period of social talk. What differs from culture to culture is how many minutes you spend chatting before moving to business. As a general rule, the more relationship-based the society, the more social conversation surrounds the task. While an Australian may invest a minute or so in personal talk with a colleague, a Mexican is much more likely to spend several long minutes on the social preliminaries before getting down to business.

In strongly relationship-based societies, such as many African and Middle Eastern cultures, the balance of social talk to business talk may tip heavily to the former. Sheldon Blake learned this well after years of working among Saudis in Jeddah:

> If I need to discuss business with a Saudi Arabian client or contact who I haven't spoken to in a while, I will make a call today just to reestablish the social connection. It would be embarrassing, and my counterpart would likely feel it abrupt or inappropriate, for me to call to discuss business, given that we haven't spoken in a while. After we have had a good chat and have reestablished a social connection, then I can call again a few days later and this time introduce the business task. This is considered a respectful approach in the Saudi culture.

When in doubt, the best strategy may be to simply let the other person lead. Relax, put your feet up, and start the call with the idea that you might spend several long minutes just catching up before the business talk starts. And then let the other person decide when enough is enough. Initiate the social, ignore your gut reaction, and listen for their cues.

As with phone calls, the standard amount of social content included in an e-mail also differs from one culture to another. If you come from a culture where a lot of social content is the norm, your task-based colleagues may feel as if you are hemming and hawing down the page. If you come from a culture where people jump right to business content, your e-mails can come across as rude or even aggressive. Just as when you are on the phone, follow the other person's lead. Research suggests that the more you mimic the other person's e-mail style, the more likely your collaborator is to respond positively to you.[4]

Jaroslav Bokowski, a Polish manager who worked in the IT department of the French multinational Saint Gobain, gave me this simple and effective example as to how to follow this rule:

> When I went to present at a conference in India, I noticed that, when the Indian organizers e-mailed me, there was always a short and friendly yet formal preamble, such as, "Greetings of the day. I hope this mail finds you in best of health and spirits." Well, in Poland, we certainly wouldn't begin an e-mail in this manner, but I thought "Why not?" and responded in kind.

When you are working face-to-face, socializing before getting down to business may come more naturally then when communication via phone or e-mail. But when you are busy and trying to figure out how to spend your precious moments, understanding when to invest in a long, friendly discussion and when to get right down to business is key. You might think you are saving a few minutes by cutting out the chitchat, only to find out later that a lot of time has been wasted because you didn't establish the appropriate social connection up front.

I had one entertaining example of this while running the first of many sessions for a group of senior executives from the New York Stock Exchange Euronext. When I described the Trusting scale, Sarah Teebone, one of the most senior women in the company, began loudly calling out, "Ding, ding, ding!" I turned to Teebone, and she explained in a strong New York accent:

> Bells are ringing in my head. I just now understood something that has happened several times over the last two years. On several occasions, managers from our French and Portuguese offices have requested one-on-one meetings with me while they are in New York. But then, when they arrive in my office, they don't have anything specific they need to talk about. After a minute or two of social talk, I start to wonder why they wanted to meet with me, and on several occasions I have asked, "What can I do for you?" To which they've replied, "I just wanted to say hello and get to know you, as we will be working together in the future."
>
> I try to be cordial. But I admit that I am thinking, "Well, okay. Here I am. Feel free to let me know if you need something. Now if you don't mind I have a few calls I need to make."
>
> Later, when e-mailing employees in Paris, I have often had the experience that people don't respond to my e-mails. I hadn't made the connection, but in considering it now, I realize that this happens only when I haven't established a relationship with that person.

Teebone laughed: "The next time I take a trip to Europe I am going to set up a few 'Just to get to know you' meetings and see what happens."

The chances are good that Teebone will discover that the time she devotes to "just saying hello" to her European colleagues will pay dividends the next time she has a business problem she needs help addressing. Trust is like insurance—it's an investment you need to make up front, before the need arises.

# 7

## The Needle, Not the Knife

Disagreeing Productively

One of my childhood memories is listening with my family to the popular American radio show, Garrison Keillor's *A Prairie Home Companion*. Keillor's deep baritone voice is still heard Saturday afternoons on hundreds of National Public Radio stations as he makes gentle fun of Minnesotans (and just about everyone else).

For years, one of the regular skits on Keillor's show was about the French chef, Maurice, the proprietor of the mythical Café Boeuf, who sees any customer as a potential verbal sparring partner. My favorite sketch involves Keillor calling to make a reservation at the Café Boeuf, only to be questioned vigorously by Maurice (in a ridiculously fake French accent, of course). What will Keillor be wearing? How can Maurice be sure that Keillor's tie will work with the restaurant's wallpaper? The more Keillor explains his sartorial choices, the more passionately Maurice questions and challenges him. It was through these sketches that I was first introduced to the image of the French as inveterate debaters.

When I moved to France, this stereotype was echoed in the daily news. Strikes and demonstrations seemed to be part of the social fabric, triggered by everything from an increase in college tuition to a proposed change in pension plans. But I really didn't experience the French love of debate on a personal level until one evening when I was invited with my (French) husband Eric to a dinner party at the home of Hélène Durand, a friend from Eric's school days.

Hélène and her husband lived near a golf course west of Paris. There were four couples around the table. All were French, except for me. As the dinner progressed, the group was laughing and getting along beautifully, with Hélène and her best friend Juliette entertaining everyone with funny tales about their mishaps on the golf course that afternoon.

But then, halfway into the meal, something unfortunate happened—or so I thought, from my American perspective. Juliette and Hélène got into a big argument over whether the town's annual golf event, which occurs every spring practically in Hélène's backyard, was a good thing or a bad one. Hélène declared fervently that she was *"totalement contre"* (completely against) the golf tournament. Juliette interrupted: *"Hélène, tu dis ça parce que tu es égoïste. Moi, je suis pour!"* ("You say that because you are selfish. I am all for it!"). The other guests began to take sides. Voices were rising and hands were waving.

Now, in my own American culture, this type of debate at the dinner table is a very bad sign. It would likely result in someone—perhaps several someones—leaving the room in a huff, slamming the door, and not returning. So I was growing increasingly uncomfortable when Juliette looked directly at me and said, "Well, Erin, what do you think?"

Having absolutely no desire to become embroiled in the debate and offend at least one of my new friends, I found my answer very quickly: "I have no opinion." And to my utter surprise, within a few minutes, the topic changed to who was going where for the upcoming holidays—with no hard feelings whatsoever. I watched in bafflement as Juliette and Hélène went arm in arm to the kitchen to get coffee, their laughter ringing through the apartment, best friends as always.

Of course, a disagreement at the dinner table can happen in just about any culture. But the fact that Hélène and Juliette could engage in such spirited public battle with no apparent impact on their friendship marks the episode as distinctly cultural.

Now think for a moment how a scene like this might play out in a business setting. Imagine the confusion that might arise among a team of people from varying cultures with dramatically different attitudes toward open disagreement. Uncomfortable? Unsettling? To say the least.

## CONFRONTATION: LOSS OF FACE OR SPIRITED DEBATE?

Li Shen, a young Chinese manager, eagerly accepted a job as a marketing manager for French multinational L'Oréal after earning her MBA at a prestigious European institution. Working at L'Oréal's Shanghai office, Shen's excellent English and acceptable French gave her a feeling of confidence when working with her European colleagues. Shen recalls, "I hadn't actually registered the cultural gap between myself and my French colleagues. After all, I studied for several years abroad, and I am much more international than most people in China. I like to feel I am able to easily move from one cultural arena to another."

After a few months, Shen was invited to come to Paris and present her ideas about how to tailor a marketing campaign to the Chinese market. "The company invested a lot in bringing me to the meeting, so I prepared my presentation tirelessly," she recalls. "I spent all thirteen hours of the plane ride from Shanghai rehearsing each slide so that my points would be polished and convincing."

There were twelve people in the meeting, and Shen was the only non-European in the group. Shen's ideas were clear and her preparation had been meticulous. But she was taken aback by the challenges thrown at her by her French colleagues. "It started with a question about why I had chosen to change a specific color in a print ad. As I explained my rationale, various members of the group began to challenge and question my decisions." Shen felt attacked and humiliated. "But mostly I felt upset with myself," she says. "They obviously did not feel that I was the marketing expert that I claimed to be." Shen did her best to keep her voice steady through the presentation, but she admits, "In truth, I was almost in tears."

When the meeting finally ended, Shen gathered her things quickly and made a dash for the door. But before she could escape, she had a surprise. "Several of the participants, the very ones who had just challenged me in front of the group, came up to congratulate me," she says. "They commented on how polished and interesting my presentation was. And at that moment, I realized I was much more Chinese than I had thought."

The concept that the Chinese call *mianzi*, or "face," exists in all societies, but with varying levels of importance. When you present yourself to others, you offer a persona that reflects what you publicly claim to be. For example, when I address a group of international executives, I present myself as a professor specializing in cross-cultural management, implicitly claiming expertise and skill at leading large groups of executives. So if a participant publicly suggests that I don't know what I am talking about—that my expertise is scanty and my leadership skills are weak—I "lose face," experiencing a sort of public shame.

In Confucian societies like China, Korea, and Japan, preserving group harmony by saving face for all members of the team is of utmost importance. Confucius preached a model of five constant relationships governing how the parent should behave to the child, the older sibling to the younger, the older friend to the younger friend, the husband to the wife, and the ruler to the subject. Under this model, group harmony exists when everyone plays his prescribed role and reinforces the roles of others. To suggest that others in the group are not living up to the expectations of their role leads to a loss of face and a disturbance of societal order.

Raised in this cultural setting, Shen was shocked by the willingness of her French colleagues to challenge her ideas in a public forum. As she puts it, "In China, protecting another person's face is more important than stating what you believe is correct."

Other Asian cultures—especially those of Japan, Indonesia and Thailand—are even more uncomfortable with direct disagreement than the Chinese. Once, when conducting a program with Toshiba Westinghouse, I asked the Japanese participants why their culture made such strong efforts to avoid confrontation. I received the following response from Hirotake Tokunaga a few days later:

> Pick up a Japanese 10,000-yen and you will see the face of Prince Shotuku, who developed the first Japanese written constitution. Prince Shotuku's Seventeen-Article Constitution begins, "Harmony should be valued and quarrels should be avoided." This sentence is deeply etched in Japanese people's minds. Therefore, in Japan we strive to create harmony with others, and we believe disagreement is a clear path to breaking harmony. It is considered deeply impolite to challenge or refute another person's point of view openly or publicly. Even the slightest deviation from the other person's perspective must be made by the subtlest hint rather than boldly or argumentatively.
>
> In Western countries, everyone is expected to have a different idea from everyone else. In Japan, it is considered more

important to avoid saying anything that might offend or disturb the harmony of those involved in the discussion and to always defer to the person of highest rank or status.

After returning to China, Shen spoke to several European colleagues about what had happened at her presentation in Paris. "One of my French teammates explained that students in the French school system are taught to disagree openly." As you may recall from our chapter on persuading, students in the French school system are taught to reason via thesis, antithesis, and synthesis, first building up one side of the argument, then the opposite side of the argument, before coming to a conclusion. Consequently, French businesspeople intuitively conduct meetings in this fashion, viewing conflict and dissonance as bringing hidden contradictions to light and stimulating fresh thinking. As Shen's colleague explained to her, "We make our points passionately. We like to disagree openly. We like to say things that shock. With confrontation, you reach excellence, you have more creativity, and you eliminate risk."

Based on the examples we've seen so far, you won't be surprised to learn that France falls on the confrontational side of the Disagreeing scale and that Japan is on the side that favors avoiding confrontation (Figure 7.1). The United States (and other Anglo-Saxon speaking countries) fall somewhere between these two extremes.

To begin to assess where your own culture falls on this scale, ask yourself the question, "If someone in my culture disagrees strongly with my idea, does that suggest they are disapproving of *me* or just of the *idea*?" In more confrontational cultures, it seems quite natural to attack someone's opinion without attacking that person. In avoid-confrontation societies, these two things are tightly interconnected.

## FIGURE 7.1. DISAGREEING

| Israel Germany Denmark Australia | US | Sweden India China | Indonesia |
|---|---|---|---|
| France Russia Spain Italy | UK | Brazil Mexico Peru Ghana | Japan |
| Netherlands | | Singapore Saudi Arabia | Thailand |

Confrontational ──────────────────────────────► Avoids confrontation

.............................................................................

**Confrontational**     Disagreement and debate are positive for the team or organization. Open confrontation is appropriate and will not negatively impact the relationship.

**Avoids confrontation**     Disagreement and debate are negative for the team or organization. Open confrontation is inappropriate and will break group harmony or negatively impact the relationship.

## CONFRONTATION VERSUS EMOTIONAL EXPRESSIVENESS

Some who have experience working with people from the Netherlands, Denmark, or Germany may be surprised to find these cultures positioned so close to the French on the left-hand side of the Disagreeing scale. After all, people from these northern European cultures are generally considered to be reserved in their expression of emotions. By the same token, a Mexican or Saudi Arabian might be surprised to see the right-hand positions of her culture on the scale. As one Mexican participant in one of my programs remarked, "When a Mexican is angry, that anger will pour out of him. We can't hide how we feel." Isn't it logical that a cultural readiness to express emotions openly would be correlated with a similar willingness to express disagreement?

There's no doubt that some cultures are more emotionally expressive than others. In a study conducted by researchers Shahid, Krahmer, and Swerts at the University of Tilberg in the Netherlands, Dutch and Pakistani children were photographed while playing a card game. The photos were then shown to a group of seventy-two Dutch adults, who had to decide whether each pair of children in a given photo had won or lost the card game.[1]

The Dutch judges did a far better job of sorting winners from losers when looking at photos of Pakistani children than with Dutch children. A glance at some sample photos shows why (see Figure 7.2). Although all the children are emotionally expressive, the Pakistani children are far more demonstrative in their facial

**FIGURE 7.2.**

**TOP ROW: PAKISTANI CHILDREN PLAYING IN PAIRS**

8-year-olds winning                8-year-olds losing

8-year-olds winning                8-year-olds losing

**BOTTOM ROW: DUTCH CHILDREN PLAYING IN PAIRS**

expressions and body language than the Dutch children. Other studies have found similar differences among other world cultures.

But emotional expressiveness is not the same thing as comfort in expressing open disagreement. In some emotionally expressive cultures, such as Spain and France, people also express disagreement openly. But in other emotionally expressive cultures, such as Peru and the Philippines, people strongly avoid open

**FIGURE 7.2. (CONTINUED)**

**TOP ROW: PAKISTANI CHILDREN PLAYING IN PAIRS**

12-year-olds winning          12-year-olds losing

12-year-olds winning          12-year-olds losing

**BOTTOM ROW: DUTCH CHILDREN PLAYING IN PAIRS**

disagreement since there is a good chance it will lead to a break in the relationship.

To understand how these two cultural patterns interact with one another, it's necessary to map the Disagreeing scale against a second scale that measures how emotionally expressive a culture is. The result is a four-quadrant matrix (Figure 7.3).

Quadrants A and D are pretty straightforward. In Quadrant A, emotions pour out—and this includes the emotions associated with disagreement, which can be expressed with little likelihood of relationships being harmed. Israel, France, Greece, Spain, and to a lesser degree Italy all follow this easy-to-read pattern. In Quadrant D, on the other hand, emotions are expressed more subtly—and disagreements are expressed more softly. Most Asian cultures fall into this quadrant; so, to a lesser degree, do a few European cultures, such as Sweden.

**FIGURE 7.3.**

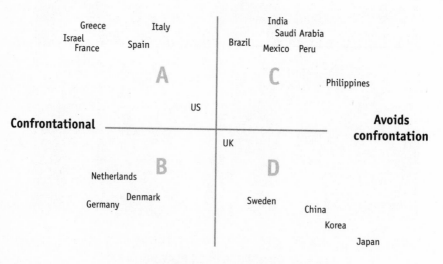

Quadrants B and C are somewhat more complicated and require a little more explanation.

Quadrant B, which houses countries like Germany and the Netherlands, includes cultures that are generally *not* emotionally expressive, yet see debate and disagreement the way the French do—as a critical step on the path to truth.

When I began consulting for DaimlerChrysler in 2002, distrust between the two historic divisions of the corporation ran deep, with many Daimler executives proclaiming publicly that they "would never drive a Chrysler." But when I welcomed a group of thirty German and American DaimlerChrysler executives into my classroom to discuss the differences between their two cultures, the tensions were not apparent. On the contrary, the group worked hard to create an atmosphere of cohesion and friendliness, with the Germans speaking impeccable English, several of the Americans practicing their German, and members of each group humbly cracking jokes at their own expense. The training session seemed to be going quite well—until I introduced the Evaluating scale late in the first morning.

When I explained that Americans are generally less direct with negative feedback than Germans, Dirk Firnhaber, one of the Germans, promptly interjected, "I totally disagree," and went on to cite several personal experiences as counterexamples. A second German colleague chimed in with his own stories in support of Firnhaber, and when I demurred, the two Germans pushed back, defending their perspective vigorously.

During the lunch break, Ben Campbell, one of the American participants, who had been virtually silent all morning, came up to me. He was visibly frustrated. "I don't get it," he said. "The Germans signed up for this course. No one is forcing them to attend. And they pay a lot of money to learn from you. They know your expertise and experience. Why do they have to constantly disagree with you?"

While we were speaking, Dirk approached us, having clearly overheard Ben's remarks. A bit uncomfortable, Ben turned to Dirk. "Is it cultural?" he wondered.

"I'll think about it," Dirk replied.

Sure enough, after lunch, Dirk was ready to share some thoughts about his readiness to challenge me during the morning session:

> We have this word in German, *Sachlichkeit*, which is most closely translated in English as "objectivity." With *Sachlichkeit*, we can separate someone's opinions or idea from the person expressing that idea. A German debate is a demonstration of *Sachlichkeit*. When I say "I totally disagree," I am debating Erin's position, not disapproving of her. Since we were children, we Germans have learned to exercise *Sachlichkeit*. We believe a good debate brings more ideas and information than we could ever discover without disagreement. For us, an excellent way to determine the robustness of a proposal is to challenge it.

Ben laughed:

> Yes! Sometimes I can imagine a German colleague walking into an empty room, closing the door, and starting a rational debate with himself. And it's not just about business issues. I've seen Germans arguing about American politics, immigration, all the topics that we Americans have been trained not to touch with a ten-foot pole.

Dirk responded:

Of course we do not debate issues that are irrelevant or boring! If we are challenging you, it is because we are interested. You Americans take things so personally. If your German colleagues challenge a decision made by the leader of your country, a person you support and admire, there's no need to get emotional or patriotic. Just calmly provide your perspective, in a rational manner, and you will likely find your workmate is simply interested.

This exchange vividly illustrates why the Germans (along with the Dutch and the Danish) belong on the confrontational side of the Disagreeing scale—despite the fact that German culture is less emotionally expressive than many others. If you think of your Germanic European business associates as stolid, silent types, you may be surprised when a matter of controversy arises. You are likely to find them eager to jump into the fray, since they regard disagreement not as a matter of personal emotion, but rather as a valuable intellectual exercise from which truth emerges.

By contrast, the cultures in Quadrant C, such as most Latin American cultures and some Middle Eastern cultures, are made up of people who speak with passion, yet are also sensitive and easily bruised. For people from these cultures, it is not easy to separate the opinion from the person. If you attack my idea, I feel you are attacking me also—which means I am likely to want to shy away from open disagreement lest it damage our relationship.

To make this more complicated, those from Latin American and (especially) Arabic cultures may appear as if they are fighting when they speak loudly and move their bodies expressively. But speaking with passion is not the same thing as disagreeing.

One spring, I led a seminar in Dubai for a multinational consulting firm. After completing my work, I decided to spend a couple of days enjoying the warm weather. An Emerati friend from work recommended a boutique hotel in another part of Dubai, and I made reservations for the weekend.

Friday at 5:00 p.m., I eagerly accepted a crosstown ride with one of my seminar participants, an energetic woman in her thirties named Isar Selim. We soon found ourselves stuck in crazy bottleneck traffic. Not until two hours later did we emerge onto a quieter street—at which point Selim began shouting out the window in Arabic to a traditionally dressed older man, who was crossing the road with a stack of colorful cloth in his arms. He responded in kind, and as their voices became louder and more intense, Selim got out of the car, shouting and gesticulating. I wondered what they were arguing about. Was he angry because Selim was dressed in Western clothing? Had her car run over some of his cloth? At one point, I thought the man looked ready to hit Selim with the bolt of cloth he was carrying.

Finally Selim got back in the car, waved her hand, and drove away. "What were you fighting about?" I asked timidly.

"Oh, we weren't fighting," she said matter-of-factly. "He was giving me directions to your hotel."

As this story illustrates, to place a culture on the Disagreeing scale, don't ask how emotionally people express themselves. Instead, focus on whether an open disagreement is likely to have a negative impact on a relationship. In Quadrant C cultures, emotional expression is common, but open disagreements are dangerous. In many Arabic cultures, people make extreme efforts not to offend others by expressing direct disagreement, as the ramifications for the long-term relationship could be serious.

One final complication in applying the Disagreeing scale is the position of the Chinese and Korean cultures on the avoid-confrontation side of the scale. If you have negotiated with a Chinese team and been forcefully challenged by them, or seen how confrontational Koreans may be with strangers, you may feel puzzled by this positioning.

The explanation lies in the fact that, in both Korea and China, behavior toward those with in-group status may be very different from behavior toward those with out-group status. Confucius provided very clear instructions about how to behave with people you have relationships with. But he provided almost no guidance on how to behave with strangers. In China in particular, where there is a large population and fierce competition, the relationship toward those with out-group status can be one of indifference and, in case of conflict, hostility. Thus, the very same Chinese person who shows polite and careful respect to his boss, colleagues, and clients may challenge every point made by a would-be supplier he doesn't know at all.

The strategy for succeeding in these cultures thus goes back to points made in the chapter on trusting. Take all the time necessary to build up a close trusting relationship. The time required may be considerable, and a foreigner may never achieve the same level of in-group status as a cultural insider, but a little time invested in building a personal connection can go a very long way toward establishing trust and reducing the level of confrontation you experience.

## GETTING GLOBAL TEAMS TO DISAGREE AGREEABLY

If you are leading a multicultural team, figuring out how to get all the group members to express their ideas openly and comfortably may be a challenge. Here are some strategies that can help.

First, if you're the boss, consider skipping the meeting. Depending on the cultures you are dealing with, both your seniority and age may impact others' comfort in disagreeing with you openly. In many avoid-confrontation cultures, it may be possible to disagree openly with a peer, but disagreeing with a boss, superior, or elder is taboo.

When Danish multinational pharmaceutical company Novo Nordisk purchased a new operation in Tokyo, Harald Madsen found himself collaborating with a group of Japanese marketing managers, all younger than him and junior to him in rank. Madsen scheduled a first trip to Tokyo in search of feedback from the local managers about which of his initiatives would work well locally and which they disagreed with. He hoped to get a good debate going with them, just as he would in Denmark. But Madsen's dreams of a lively sparring match and a creative exchange of ideas quickly evaporated:

> I began the first meeting by telling my Japanese colleagues that I wanted them to feel comfortable challenging my ideas so that we could be sure we had the best solution for their market. I then presented a few ideas and asked for input. Silence. I pushed the few with the best English-speaking skills, but it was impossible. I tried to get the ball rolling. Silence. I pushed them for input. A few nods of agreement and platitudes.
>
> I could not figure out how to achieve a productive discussion if the group would not debate and share differing viewpoints.

All the tools and techniques I had developed in Denmark were getting me nowhere.

Later in the same trip, over dinner one evening, Madsen asked Kazuyiki Yoshisaki—a Japanese vice president at his own level—for advice. "Here in Japan," Yoshisaki explained, "even asking another's point of view can feel confrontational in our culture. When you go around the table asking each guy on the team 'What do you think about this? What do you think about that?' that can really take them off guard. No one wants to be put on the spot in front of a bunch of people."

Advance preparation would help Japanese managers feel more comfortable sharing their opinions openly. Yoshisaki suggested that Madsen let his team know a few days before the meeting what input he needed from them, so that they could check with one another and prepare their comments.

"But the real problem," Yoshisaki commented, "is your white hair. In Japanese culture, you almost never see middle management disagreeing openly with higher management or younger people disagreeing with older people. It would be viewed as disrespectful. When you tell them your opinion and then ask what they think, they are eager to offer their support. Perhaps you think they will say, 'Dear elder vice president, I entirely disagree with you,' but they will not."

Yoshisaki suggested that Madsen avoid giving his opinion first. He also suggested that Madsen ask the team to meet without him and report back their ideas. "As long as the boss is present," Yoshisaki said, "the group will seek to find out what his opinion is and defer respectfully to him." This is a technique that's worth trying whenever you find yourself managing a team whose cultural background makes it difficult for them to speak freely in your presence.

A second strategy for eliciting opinions in an avoids-confrontation culture is to depersonalize disagreement by separating ideas from the people proposing them.

Consider for a moment the brainstorming system that is so popular in Anglo-Saxon cultures. Four or five people gather to record on a flip chart every crazy, brilliant, or downright stupid idea they can muster up. Once the paper is filled, it's difficult to remember who came up with which idea, making it easy to challenge or change an idea without attacking the person who came up with it.

Harald Madsen took this concept a step further on his next trip to Japan:

> After a presentation, instead of asking for input and expecting people to raise their hands—which I now knew from experience would not happen—I asked everybody to write as many opinions and reactions as they could on Post-it notes. During a break they put their Post-its anonymously on the main board and then, as a group, we arranged them into sets. Next, still working all together, we made lists of the positive and negative elements of each set of ideas, and finally prioritized them by voting on the most important. Each member had only three votes, so each of us really needed to make a clear choice.

Madsen found this approach to be very effective at producing the positive results of debate and disagreement without risking relationships.

A third strategy is to conduct meetings *before* the meeting. I discovered the need for this approach after attending a number of cross-cultural meetings that struck me as boring and pointless—but which participants from other cultures found interesting and valuable. Curious, I began surveying my seminar participants about what they expected from meetings. I asked:

In order for you to feel a meeting was a great success, which of the following should happen?

A.  In a good meeting, a decision is made.
B.  In a good meeting, various viewpoints are discussed and debated.
C.  In a good meeting, a formal stamp is put on a decision that has been made before the meeting.

The large majority of Americans responding to this question chose option A. The French, however, largely chose option B. And most Chinese and Japanese selected option C. In many Asian cultures, the default purpose of a meeting is to approve a decision that has already been made in informal discussions. Therefore, the most appropriate time to express your disagreement is before the meeting to an individual rather than during the meeting in front of the group.

It's relatively easy to make this cultural preference work for you. Before your next team meeting, try calling your Japanese colleague for a casual offline discussion. You are much more likely to hear a frank opinion, especially if you have already built a good relationship.

If you have a large percentage of East Asians on your global team, you may consider adopting the informal premeeting approach and encourage everyone to make one-on-one prep calls to hear opinions and reach an agreement. Then you can use your meetings to put a formal stamp on any consensus decision reached. Explain the process clearly (that is, use the "framing" tactic described in previous chapters) so that everyone understands the process explicitly. No matter what objective you choose for your own global team meetings (option A, B, or C), you can help everyone by being explicit about which method you are using.

A fourth strategy for encouraging debate among those who would otherwise shun confrontation is to adjust your language, avoiding upgraders and employing downgraders (see pages 65–67 in Chapter 2) when expressing disagreement. As you recall, an upgrader is a word that makes an opinion sound stronger, such as "absolutely," "totally," or "completely." Such words are popular in confrontational cultures. By contrast, in confrontation-avoiding cultures, people are more likely to use downgraders such as "sort of," "kind of," "slightly," or "partially." An extreme example comes from a former Thai colleague, who would express her disagreement with me by using a quadruple downgrader: "*Maybe* we could think about this *slightly* differently . . . *perhaps . . . what do you think?*"

When expressing disagreement yourself, it is not difficult to change your words slightly based on the cultural context you are working in. Sean Green, an American living and managing a team in Mexico City, describes his experience:

> After starting my assignment in Mexico, I attended several meetings during which I would disagree with a stance that one of my peers or staff members had taken. And I would voice that disagreement by saying "I don't agree with you." But in Mexican culture this level of disagreement is not acceptable, and my open expression of disagreement would effectively end the debate with no further attempt to change my point of view.
>
> I soon learned that, if I wanted to encourage team debate, it was important to use phrases like "I do not quite understand your point" and "Please explain more about why you think

that." These expressions encouraged give-and-take rather than shutting down the conversation completely.

On the other hand, if you are working with a culture that is *more* confrontational than your own, be very careful about choosing stronger words than are natural to you to express your disagreement unless you have a solid and nuanced grasp on exactly where the line is drawn between acceptable debate and inappropriate attack. I do not recommend that you begin an overseas meeting by telling your French client, "You are totally wrong," or announcing to your German supplier, "I am in absolute disagreement with your proposal." In these cultures, disagreement is expressed more directly than in some others, but that doesn't mean anything goes. It's easy to overshoot on the Disagreeing scale.

This happened to Wei Lin, a Stanford-educated accounting professor from China who became a colleague of mine at INSEAD. Lin was startled when students made classroom comments like "I don't agree with that point," which struck him as insolent and inappropriate. Add to this the fact that Lin was rather small and youthful, so that many of his Dutch, German, and Scandinavian MBA students towered over him, and Lin began to feel that the in-class disagreements amounted to a public attack on his authority.

Lin sought advice from several of his fellow professors. "They seemed to feel it was both appropriate and beneficial to have a debate with the students in the classroom," Lin recalls. "So I decided I would be just as confrontational with them as they were with me." Unfortunately, Wei Lin didn't quite understand the subtle difference between healthy debate and full-on aggression in a European context. "I was really shocked when I got the participant evaluations at the end of the semester. The students described me as hostile and angry," he says. "But I was just trying to adapt to their style."

Ultimately, Lin managed to find a happy medium:

> I found that I could have good results by allowing the students to question and disagree forcefully, while constantly reminding myself that this was a sign of engagement, not criticism. I tried to give them a comfortable space to express all their disagreements, without confronting them back. This way I remained Chinese in my own behavior—polite and striving for group harmony— but not Chinese at all in my reaction to their behavior. This seemed to work well. I developed a great relationship with my students—much closer than I used to have with my students in China, where the professor is always put up on a pedestal. Now, when I go back to China and the participants all defer to my opinions silently, I wish they would disagree with me, at least once in a while.

Particularly when working with a culture that is more confrontational than your own, adapting your style to be like them carries a big risk. Take a page from Lin's strategy book. Remind yourself that what feels aggressive in your culture may not feel so in another culture. Don't take offense if you can help yourself. But don't try to mimic a confrontational style that doesn't come naturally to you. Engage in relaxed debate or discussion without confronting back.

## "LET ME PLAY DEVIL'S ADVOCATE"

Imagine for a moment that the Durands, whom you met during the dinner party at the beginning of this chapter, were to move to your hometown. What might happen if they held a dinner party and invited you, your family, and several neighborhood friends? To be good hosts, would they need to tone down the way they disagree?

If the Durands were to move to Minnesota and settle in near my parent's home a few blocks east of Lake Calhoun, using a softer style of disagreement would certainly be one good strategy. But not the only one. Instead, Hélène Durand could encourage a lively debate about golf tournaments or anything else she found interesting by putting a frame around her words—explaining her style of disagreeing before putting it into practice.

My husband Eric was raised in the same community as Hélène and has lived for many years in both the United Kingdom and the United States—including my hometown. Although he has learned to work in both the French and Anglo-Saxon environments, he feels that for any French person working with Americans or British, the Disagreeing scale is one of the most important—and challenging. By comparison with the French, the Americans value harmony and equilibrium. Under the umbrella of their written constitution, the Bill of Rights, and the Declaration of Independence, Americans have developed a highly complex, multi-ethnic citizenry characterized by peaceful, tolerant coexistence (much of the time). As a result, Americans tend to perceive dissent as a threat to their unity. "United we stand, divided we fall," is the basis for many social interactions in the United States.

After inadvertently creating some awkward scenes in American meetings with his straightforward, French-style disagreements, Eric devised a solution:

I learned a very simple trick, perhaps obvious to someone who is British or American but not a bit obvious to me. Before expressing disagreement, I now always explain, "Let me play devil's advocate, so we can explore both sides." Most groups seem happy to do this, as long as I am clear about what I am doing and why I am doing it.

Sometimes just a few words of explanation framing your behavior can make all the difference in how your actions are perceived. Whether you are from France and living in Minnesota, or from Russia and living in Bangkok, recognizing how your approach is viewed by those around you, and taking a moment to describe what you are doing and why—perhaps with a touch of humor and humility—can greatly enhance your effectiveness.

There's a wise Bahamian proverb: "To engage in conflict, one does not need to bring a knife that cuts, but a needle that sews." As we've seen in this chapter, what sews nicely in one culture may cut in another. But with a little effort and creativity, you can find many ways to encourage and learn from alternative points of view while safeguarding valuable relationships.

# 8

## How Late Is Late?

### Scheduling and Cross-Cultural Perceptions of Time

Schedules, deadlines, time pressure . . . we are all painfully handcuffed to the notion of time. Scheduling is a state of mind that affects how you organize your day, how you run a meeting, how far you must plan in advance, and how flexible those plans are. Yet what is considered appallingly late in one culture may be acceptably on time in another.

Consider the morning you wake up to that harmonica sound from your iPhone reminding you about a meeting with a supplier on the other side of town at 9:15 a.m. . . . But your day has an unexpectedly chaotic start. Your toddler breaks a jar of raspberry jam on the floor and your older son accidentally steps in it, leading to several stressful minutes of cleanup. This is followed by a desperate search for the car keys, which finally turn up in the kitchen cupboard. You manage to drop the kids off at school just as the bells are ringing and the doors are closing. At that moment, your iPhone chimes 9:00 a.m., which means you'll be about six or seven minutes late for the important meeting—provided the crosstown traffic is no worse than usual.

What to do?

You could of course call the supplier to apologize and explain that you will be arriving exactly at 9:21. Or possibly 9:22.

Or you consider that six or seven minutes late is basically on time. You decide not to call and simply pull your car out into traffic.

And then perhaps you just don't give the time any thought at all. Whether you arrive at 9:21 or 9:22 or even 9:45, you will still be within a range of what is considered acceptably on time, and neither you nor the supplier will think much of it.

If you live in a linear-time culture like Germany, Scandinavia, the United States, or the United Kingdom, you'll probably make the call. If you don't, you risk annoying your supplier as the seconds tick on and you still haven't shown up.

On the other hand, if you live in France or northern Italy, chances are you won't feel the need to make the call, since being six or seven minutes late is within the realm of "basically on time." (If you were running twelve or fifteen minutes late, however, that would be a different story.)

And if you are from a flexible-time culture such as the Middle East, Africa, India, or South America, time may have an altogether different level of elasticity in your mind. In these societies, as you fight traffic and react to the chaos that life inevitably throws your way, it is expected that delays will happen. In this context, 9:15 differs very little from 9:45, and everybody accepts that.

When people describe those from another culture using words like *inflexible, chaotic, late, rigid, disorganized, inadaptable*, it's quite likely the scheduling dimension is the issue. And understanding the subtle, often unexpressed assumptions about time that control behaviors and expectations in various cultures can be quite challenging.

When I first moved to France, I was warned by other Americans that the French were always late. And this turned out to be partially true, though the impact on my daily work was small. For example, shortly after arriving in Paris, I arranged to visit a human resources manager specializing in expatriate assignments, in one of the glass towers of La Défense (the Paris corporate business district). Arriving carefully at 9:55 a.m. for my 10:00 a.m. appointment, I practiced my rusty French nervously in my head. The woman I was scheduled to meet, Sandrine Guegan, was a longtime client of the firm and knew my boss well. He had assured me that Ms. Guegan would welcome me warmly.

The receptionist called Madame Guegan at precisely 10:00 a.m. and, after a second with her on the phone, said to me politely, *"Patientez s'il vous plaît"* (wait patiently please). So I perched myself carefully on the big leather couch and pretended I was looking at a newspaper while I waited patiently for five minutes. But at 10:07 I was not feeling very patient. Had I gotten the time of the meeting wrong? Was there some unavoidable emergency? And at 10:10 . . . was the meeting going to take place at all? Madame Guegan stepped out of the elevator at 10:11, and, without a word of apology for her tardiness, she welcomed me warmly. After many years of working in both the United States and France, I can now confirm that in most cases you get about ten more minutes' leeway (to run late, start late, end late, take a tangent) in France than you would in the United States. And if you know this, in most circumstances it is really no big deal to adapt.

The first time I *really* understood the impact of the scheduling dimension came when I was working in South America. Earlier in the week, I had given a keynote speech in Denver, Colorado, to a group of approximately five hundred, mostly American, managers. The afternoon before the event, Danielle, the conference organizer, had shown me a stack of cards she would be holding in her lap during my forty-minute talk. "I'll hold up a sign every ten minutes," she explained, showing me cards that read "thirty minutes," "twenty minutes," and "ten minutes" in bold black characters. The sequence concluded with cards that read "five minutes," "two minutes," and "zero minutes." It was evident that the big black zero on the final card meant in no uncertain terms that my time was up, and, when I saw it, I was to exit the stage.

I understood Danielle perfectly. She is a typical member of my (American) tribe, and I was very comfortable with the idea of monitoring each minute carefully. My speech went beautifully, and my linear-time audience was aptly appreciative.

A few days later I was dining with Flavio Ranato, a charming older Brazilian man, in a glass-walled restaurant overlooking the lights of Brazil's fifth-largest city, Belo Horizonte. We were planning the presentation I would give the next day to a large group of South Americans. "This topic is very important to our organization," Ranato told me. "The participants will love it. Please feel free to take more time than is scheduled if you like. The group will benefit."

I didn't quite understand, as I had already tested my presentation with the IT support person, and the agenda for the conference was already printed and posted on the conference door. "I have forty-five minutes on the agenda. How much time were you thinking? Could I take sixty minutes?" I wondered out loud.

With a gentle shrug of his shoulders, Ranato responded, "Of course, take the time you need."

Uncertain about his meaning I confirmed, "Great, I will take sixty minutes," and Ranato nodded in agreement. I went back to my hotel room and adapted my presentation to a sixty-minute time slot.

The next day at the conference, I noticed immediately that the agenda on the door still said I had forty-five minutes. A bit unnerved, I sought out Ranato in the crowd. "I just want to make sure I understood correctly," I said. "Did you want me to take forty-five or sixty minutes for my presentation this morning?"

Ranato laughed a little, as if my behavior was unusual. "Do not worry, Erin," he tried to reassure me. "They will love it. Please take whatever time you need."

"I will take sixty minutes," I articulated again.

When my presentation began (after a number of unanticipated delays), the group responded as Ranato had predicted. They were boisterously appreciative, waving their arms to ask questions and provide examples during the question period at the end of my talk. Carefully watching the large clock at the back of the room, I ended my session after sixty-five minutes. I was a few minutes late as one question ran longer than I had expected.

Ranato approached me. "It was great, just as I hoped. But you ended so early!"

Early? I was really confused. "I thought I was supposed to take sixty minutes, and I took sixty-five," I ventured.

"You could have certainly gone longer! They were loving it!" Ranato insisted.

Later that evening, Ranato and I had an enlightening discussion about our mutual incomprehension.

"I didn't want to use any extra moment of your group's time without getting explicit permission," I explained. "You gave me sixty minutes. To me, it would be disrespectful to the group if I took more time than prescheduled without getting your permission."

"But I don't get it," Ranato responded. "In this situation, we are the customer. We are paying you to be here with us. If you see that we have more questions and would like to continue the discussion, isn't it simply good customer service to extend the presentation in order to answer our questions and meet our needs?"

I was confused. "But if you have not explicitly told me that I can take another fifteen minutes, how do I know that is what you want?"

Ranato looked at me curiously, as it started to dawn on him how much of a foreigner I was. "They were so obviously interested and engaged. Couldn't you tell?"

I was beginning to realize how enormous the impact of differing attitudes toward time can be. The assumptions Ranato and I made about scheduling caused us to have contrasting definitions of "good customer service." The story underscores the importance of understanding how the people you work with think about time—and adjusting your expectations accordingly.

## STUDYING CULTURE TILL THE COWS COME HOME

Anthropologist Edward T. Hall was one of the first researchers to explore differences in societal approaches to time. In *The Dance of Life: The Other Dimension of Time*, Hall referred to *monochronic* (M-time) cultures and *polychronic* (P-time) cultures. M-time cultures view time as tangible and concrete: "We speak of time as being saved, spent, wasted, lost, made up, crawling, killing and running out. These metaphors must be taken seriously. M-time scheduling is used as a classification system that orders life. These rules apply to everything except death."[1]

By contrast, P-time cultures take a flexible approach to time, involvement of people, and completion of transactions: "Appointments are not taken seriously and, as a consequence, are frequently broken as it is more likely to be considered a point rather than a ribbon in the road. . . . An Arab will say 'I will see you before one hour' or 'I will see you after two days.'" In other words, a person who lives in P-time will suggest a general approximate meeting slot in the coming future without nailing down the exact moment that meeting will take place.

When I worked as a Peace Corps volunteer in Botswana (a P-time culture), I used to feel puzzled that a local teacher at my school would tell me "I am coming now," but twenty minutes later I would still be waiting with no sign of that person's arrival. Later, I learned that if someone was actually coming right away, they would say "I am coming now, now." That second "now" made all the difference.

In the wake of Hall's work, psychologist Robert Levine began meticulously observing and analyzing various cultural approaches to clocks.[2] He noted that some cultures measure time in five-minute intervals, while other cultures barely use clocks and instead schedule their day on what Levine calls "event time": before lunch, after sunrise, or in the case of the locals in Burundi, "when the cows come home."

Of course, a business manager in any country in the world is more likely to wear a wristwatch than to tell time by the sunset or by passing cows. But the way individuals experience the time shown by the hands on the watch still differs dramatically from one society to the next.

## RELATIONSHIPS: A KEY TO UNDERSTANDING THE SCHEDULING SCALE

As with the other cultural scales we've examined in this book, the Scheduling scale is profoundly affected by a number of historic factors that shape the ways people live, work, think, and interact with one another. Positions on the Scheduling scale are partially affected by how fixed and reliable, versus dynamic and unpredictable, daily life is in a particular country.

If you live in Germany, you probably find that things pretty much go according to plan. Trains are reliable; traffic is manageable; systems are dependable; government rules are clear and enforced more or less consistently. You can probably schedule your entire year on the assumption that your environment is not likely to interfere greatly with your plans.

There's a clear link between this cultural pattern and Germany's place in history as one of the first countries in the world to become heavily industrialized. Imagine being a factory worker in the German automotive industry. If you arrive at work four minutes late, the machine for which you are responsible gets started late, which exacts a real, measurable financial cost. To this day, the perception of time in Germany is partially rooted in the early impact of the industrial revolution, where factory work required the labor force to be on hand and in place at a precisely appointed moment.

In other societies—particularly in the developing world—life centers around the fact of constant change. As political systems shift and financial systems alter, as traffic surges and wanes, as monsoons or water shortages raise unforeseeable challenges, the successful managers are those who have developed the ability to ride out the changes with ease and flexibility. Scheduling things in advance is fine—but only if the time horizon is forty-eight hours or less.

For example, if you are a farmer in the Nigerian countryside, most of the farmwork is done by people, and you likely have few machines. In this environment, it doesn't matter much if you start work at 7:00 or 7:12 or even 7:32. What matters is that your work structure is flexible enough to adapt with changes in the natural environment, and that you have invested in the critical relationships needed to keep your workers loyal in times of drought or flooding, erosion or insect infestation. In this environment, productivity and profit are directly linked to the flexibility and the relationships of the person in charge.

Indeed, the importance of relationships seems to be a key to understanding the Scheduling scale. It's only logical that if relationships are a priority, you will put them before the clock. Thus it's natural that cultures that put a premium on relationship building tend, with a few exceptions, to fall on the flexible-time side of the Scheduling scale (see Figure 8.1).

As usual, all positions on the scale should be considered in relative terms. Germans may complain bitterly about the British lack of punctuality, and Indians often feel the French are rigid with their scheduling. However, Germanic, Anglo-Saxon, and Northern European countries generally fall on the linear-time side of the scale. Latin cultures (both Latin European and Latin American) tend to fall on the flexible-time side, with Middle Eastern and many African cultures on the far right. Asian cultures are scattered

### FIGURE 8.1. SCHEDULING

| Germany | Japan | Netherlands | | Poland | | Spain | Italy | Brazil | China | | Saudi Arabia |
| Switzerland | Sweden | US | UK | Czech Republic | France | | Russia | Mexico | | | India | Nigeria |
| | | Denmark | | | | | | | Turkey | | | Kenya |

← **Linear-time**                                                    **Flexible-time** →

**Linear-time**  Project steps are approached in a sequential fashion, completing one task before beginning the next. One thing at a time. No interruptions. The focus is on the deadline and sticking to the schedule. Emphasis is on promptness and good organization over flexibility.

**Flexible-time**  Project steps are approached in a fluid manner, changing tasks as opportunities arise. Many things are dealt with at once and interruptions accepted. The focus is on adaptability, and flexibility is valued over organization.

on this scale. Japan is linear-time, but China and (especially) India practice flexible-time.

When you work with people from varying cultures, you find that the scheduling dimension impacts a remarkable number of aspects of daily life, from how meetings are run to how people wait in line.

## A LINE IS NOT A LINE: QUEUING IN STOCKHOLM VERSUS SWARMING IN INDORE

It was a December morning in Stockholm—pitch-dark and very cold. I was going to meet with a client at the Swedish company Seco Tools, whose office was close to the route of bus #42. As I waited, I barely noticed the other people gathered at the bus stop, since I was mostly focused on moving my legs briskly in a vain attempt to stay warm. So when the bus pulled up, I was eager to get on. The woman closest to the door got on first, and then I stepped forward, happy to follow her. However, although I had been oblivious to the loose queue my fellow passengers had formed, I could scarcely miss the angry coughs they directed my way when I boarded before them.

Cutting in line—even inadvertently—is a cultural crime in Sweden. This rule is a natural outgrowth of the linear-time belief in managing items one at a time, in proper order—including people who are waiting in line.

By contrast, before traveling to India several students had explained to me the "evergreen tree culture" of waiting one's turn. When it is necessary for a line to form, for example when waiting to purchase a ticket, some eager individuals will form the initial trunk of a tree. Then, when the trunk begins to look too long to some, a few individuals will create their own lines by standing next to, say, the fifth person in the trunk and implicitly suggesting that others line up behind them. This process continues until you have a human evergreen tree, a single-file trunk of people waiting with restless branches sprouting and growing on both sides.[3]

This, at least, was the preparation I had received before my trip. My own experience suggests that Indian queues can be even more flexible than the "evergreen tree theory" implies.

I had just spent two days in Indore, the most populous city in central India, working with a group of undergraduate students at the Indian Institute of Planning and Management. When I arrived at the check-in counter for my flight from Indore Airport, I carefully positioned myself at the front of the line in order to avoid any branch-sprouting.

Soon, however, dozens of other passengers began to arrive, swarming behind me. Within minutes, I was surrounded by people with questions, lost tickets, and oversized bags. One woman put her ticket on the counter next to mine, explaining some urgent problem related to the name on the ticket. An older gentleman caught the check-in woman's attention by describing in Hindi some urgent matter to do with his bag. The kind woman behind the counter began tending to several customers at once, making phone calls, printing new tickets, and answering questions from people pushing forward on my left and my right.

Somewhat to my surprise, all of the customers' needs were met and we departed more or less on schedule.

That evening in New Delhi, I regaled my Indian host with the difference between waiting in line in Indore versus Stockholm. "You are right," he laughed.

We are more flexible in India. Because we grew up in a society where currency wasn't always stable and governments could change regulations on a whim, we learned to value flexibility over linear planning. But Europeans and Americans are more rigid. They expect us to work by carefully closing one box before opening the next. Like your idea that only one person in the queue should be treated at a time, with no interruptions.

I was learning that flexible-time cultures, like India, tend to emphasize leaving many boxes open and working on all of them simultaneously. One thing at a time? That may be common sense in Stockholm, but not in Indore.

## A MEETING IS LIKE WAITING IN A LINE

The differences between lines in Sweden and lines in India reflect broader differences between linear-time cultures and flexible-time cultures.

Consider, for example, a simple business meeting. In the United States, the United Kingdom, Scandinavia, or Germany, you're likely to find that all parties attending the meeting share the assumption that a meeting should look like a line. Accordingly, an agenda is set out ahead of time explaining, in the form of a list, exactly what time the meeting will start and what subjects will be discussed in what order. Sometimes an actual number of minutes are allotted to each topic so that the meeting can end at a preset time.

If an attendee should try to "hijack" the meeting by bringing up some topic *not* found on the agenda, one linear-time participant is likely to interrupt, saying, "This is not on the agenda, so let's take this offline and discuss it at a break," or "Let's park this until another time," or "Can we put this on the agenda for next week?" or perhaps an exasperated "People! A little discipline, please!"

What's more, in a linear-time culture, people in a meeting are supposed to behave as if in a Swedish line. You should not be talking to your neighbor at the same time someone else is talking. You should not be taking cell phone calls on the sidelines. The group will take scheduled "bio breaks," so please don't leave and re-enter the room. For those on linear time, any behavior that distracts from the predefined task at hand is just plain rude.

But a meeting in a flexible-time culture like those found in South America, parts of Europe, Africa, and the Middle East is more like an evergreen tree. An agenda with a meeting start time and a topic will probably be circulated before the meeting. This will serve as the trunk of the tree. But there's no expectation that the meeting will progress in a linear manner. What seemed like a priority last week when the agenda was crafted is not necessarily the priority right now—so discussion may branch off in a new direction. Other branches may sprout as some members have urgent phone calls that take them in and out of the meeting. Or subgroups may form within the room to discuss timely subjects linked in some way to the main meeting trunk.

In flexible-time cultures, it seems clear that the most productive meetings grow in unpredictable ways, and the effective manager is flexible and professional enough to capitalize on priorities and changing needs as they arise. Interruptions, agenda changes, and frequent shifts in direction are seen as natural and necessary.

## WAITING FOR A SIGN FROM THE MOON: THE STYLE-SWITCHING APPROACH TO SCHEDULING CHALLENGES

As you might expect, the scheduling dimension also impacts the way we plan our time and how fixed or flexible those plans are felt to be.

When Dr. Ahmed Acidah, an articulate and experienced human resources executive from a Nigerian bank, applied to attend our one-week Global Virtual Teams program at INSEAD, I hesitated. Normally participants attending this program have teams dispersed across many countries. But Acidah had just two nationalities on his team—Nigerian and German. However, we did accept Acidah into the program, and it turned out he had enough experience with cross-cultural misunderstandings between these two nationalities to fill a year's worth of discussion.

During the program, Acidah explained one of the challenges he faced:

> The Germans plan everything not just weeks, but months in advance. Last week, three months before a conference I will attend in Germany, I received an e-mail asking me to choose, from three options, what I want to have for dinner at the conference opener on April 6. Now let me ask you, how can I be expected to know today, a day in January, what I am going to want to eat on April 6? But this is no joke. If you don't check the box, schedule your meal choice, and return it by the stated date, someone will start hunting you by e-mail.

Acidah's Nigerian staff was in a full-fledged revolt against this approach. The Germans, their calendars filled with meetings scheduled months earlier, wanted to get the team meetings for the next six months on the calendar now; that way they felt assured the meetings would take place and projects would move forward as expected. The Nigerians were caught between not wanting to create a fuss over a mere calendar invitation, and knowing from experience that trouble would ensue if they committed now and were unable to follow through later. Acidah continued:

What these Germans do not understand is that things are always changing in Nigeria. I can't possibly schedule a meeting three months from today because it is impossible to know what will have changed. I am from the Muslim part of Nigeria, and where I live you don't even know when the holiday is going to start until the Supreme Leader looks at the moon and says that the holiday starts now. If I don't know which days will be a holiday, how can I possibly know at which moment two months and seven days from now I will be available to talk on the phone?

My German colleagues don't get it. They want me to tell them weeks in advance if I will be available on Tuesday, June 24— and if I am not available when that day rolls around, they take offense.

This small example illustrates the difficulties of developing realistic schedules when working internationally. One culture tells time by when the cows come home. Another schedules meetings based on the Supreme Leader's moon analysis. A speaker from Minnesota stops speaking the moment the zero card pops up, leaving her Brazilian host baffled about her refusal to satisfy an audience hungry for additional insights.

A first strategy for dealing effectively with the Scheduling scale is to increase your own ability to work in different ways. Style switching is an essential skill for today's global manager.

Mario Mota, a Brazilian from Rio de Janeiro working for the World Bank, tells how he learned to switch styles in regard to a simple but vexing scheduling problem:

As a child, I learned from my mother that when invited to dinner, it is inappropriate to arrive at the time the host has asked you to come. Doing so will ultimately end with the hosts running frantically around the house to put things in order and will cause unnecessary stress for everyone. The best time to arrive is fifteen minutes after the stated time—or later—so the hosts will be ready and relaxed, and everyone will enjoy the evening.

I will never forget the first time, as a young manager, I was invited to my American boss's house for dinner. My boss and his wife invited me as well as the four other members of my team for 6:00 p.m. and I carefully arrived at 6:35. "What happened?" the worried hosts asked as they opened the door. "Did you get lost? Or stuck in traffic?" Everyone was waiting for me and the table was already set. What a humiliation!

Fortunately, the Scheduling scale is one of the easier scales to adapt to. It only took one awkward dinner for Mota to learn the proper time to arrive when invited to dinner in an American household. The next time, he recalls, "I arrived five minutes before the stated start time, parked my car around the corner and watched the clock carefully. At 5.59 p.m., I left the car and at six o'clock I rang the doorbell. My hosts were expecting me."

Sometimes style switching is this easy: Learn what works best in that culture and do things the way they do them. However, understanding the cultural nuances and gauging them precisely can sometimes be challenging. Mota offers another story:

Although I worked hard during my career on becoming more culturally agile, I have learned that, if you try adapting your style, three times out of five you will miss the mark on the first try.

I was running a meeting in Germany a few weeks ago. I know the Germans are even more focused on punctuality than the Americans, but I didn't really know *how* punctual that meant. My presentation was supposed to end at 2:00 p.m. I was watching the clock carefully. And at 2:02 I was ready to wrap up, when one of the German participants asked a question that required a detailed answer. And I said something very un-Brazilian. I said, "This is a very interesting question, but I'm afraid time is up." I found out later from the organizers that the Germans were put off by my rigid approach. They felt I was inflexible.

My Brazilian way would have been to answer the question in front of everyone, stretching the meeting longer. Since I knew that my natural strategy wasn't the best one for this context, I defaulted to something that came off as abrupt and unprofessional.

Later, I gave it some thought, and I realized all the simple and obvious ways I could have better handled the situation. I could have done like the Americans do and asked to take the question "offline," meaning we will end the official part of the meeting now and discuss the question one-on-one afterward. Or I could have said I'd be happy to answer the question for anyone who wanted to stay longer.

Style switching sounds very simple, but it takes a lot of trial and error to understand the subtleties and to get them right. You have to try, miss the mark, try again, and gradually find you are becoming more and more competent.

Complicating style switching is the fact that each culture has its own peculiarities and apparent contradictions. Cam Johnson was raised in Michigan and lived in Tokyo for two years before moving to Beijing. In Japan, he became aware of the enormous importance placed on punctuality—even when it comes to events where punctuality is ignored in the United States. Cam recalls, "I took my teenage son to an Eminem rap concert in Chiba at the Makuhari Messe. The concert was scheduled to start at 8:00 p.m. In other countries, a rap concert starts thirty, sixty, ninety minutes late. Not in Tokyo. We showed up eleven minutes late because of traffic, and my son missed eleven minutes of the show."

When Cam moved his family to Beijing, he initially believed that the Chinese would take a similar approach to time. Little by little, however, the differences between the Chinese and Japanese scheduling systems became clear to him:

> In Chinese culture, punctuality is a virtue, and if you arrive late for a meeting you should definitely apologize for your tardiness. But any similarity in approach to time between the Chinese and Japanese stops there. The Japanese are highly organized planners. They are definitely more organized than they are flexible. In China, everything happens immediately, without preplanning. The Chinese are the kings of flexibility. This is a culture where people don't think about tomorrow or next week; they think about right now.
>
> For example, I had to call an electrician because my TV was broken. Within five minutes of my hanging up the phone, he was knocking at my door. When I had a clogged drain, I called the plumber and he showed up a few minutes later. Now I know that, when there is a problem with something, I'd better be ready for someone to come in and fix it as soon as I pick up the phone.
>
> Reactivity is key here, but that also means that plans that are made in advance are considered flexible. The Chinese will often pop in to see you with no appointment. This used to make me angry. I felt they didn't respect my time. Can't they send a simple e-mail in advance so I can be ready for them when they arrive? Do they think I don't have anything else to do? That my time is disposable?

But now that I've become a bit Chinese myself, I've learned I can do this, too. If I'm traveling in Guangzhou and I have thirty minutes to spare, I just make a quick call from a taxi and visit someone working in the area. I've come to see this system as highly flexible and efficient.

Something similar applies to meetings. In China, if you send out an advance agenda, you'll arrive to find out either that no one has read the agenda or that the meeting has been canceled. So now I call a day before to make sure the meeting is still on. And when we meet, I try to remain flexible and let things get covered in whatever order they may happen rather than trying to stick with a prearranged schedule.

The most interesting thing about hearing how Johnson learned to work with the Chinese was how he came to appreciate the strengths of the Chinese approach:

Now I look at the way my Chinese colleagues work and I just marvel at it. They are amazing at ad hoc logistics. For example, I've attended dozens of workshops in China, and not one has gone according to plan. Things change the night before: speakers, topics, even venues. But it all ends up working out. Once you understand that the Chinese are extremely flexible, everything works fine if you just do the same.

## THE FRAMING STRATEGY FOR CROSS-CULTURAL LEADERS

Style switching is a powerful approach for those who are visiting another culture—indeed, an essential one. But what if you are not the visitor? What if you are the leader in charge of a multicultural team with members who practice a variety of scheduling styles? In this situation, flexibility and open-mindedness are not enough.

It's nine o'clock on Monday morning, and my course is supposed to start. However, of the thirty-two Saudi Arabian managers who are visiting INSEAD and are scheduled to spend the day with me, only one is in the classroom—and since he is talking on the phone, I can't ask him where the rest are.

Fifteen minutes later, the group starts to trickle in, and at about 9:35 I get started. It all works fine for me. Understanding the Saudi flexible-time system, I let both my lectures and our breaks stretch a little longer, using any extra time to build relationships and get to know one another better.

The following week, I happened to have another classroom day scheduled with a group of Saudis. This time, the program director had taken steps to adjust the students' scheduling expectations. During the program introduction, he told them, "During our week together, we should all imagine we are in Switzerland. We will start on time, to the minute, and end on time, to the minute. And anyone who forgets this team culture and comes late to class will have to contribute five euros to the fund for our end-of-the- week champagne party!"

The system worked. This group of thirty-two Saudi Arabian managers were the most punctual group I have ever worked with. At nine o'clock sharp, every single student was in his seat. The only catch was that I was subject to the same rules. If I arrived late after a break or allowed my lecture to run long, I had to pay, too. That day cost me fifteen euros—but I will do better next time.

People can be remarkably adaptable when it comes to the Scheduling scale if the team leader establishes a clear and explicit team culture.

Cam Johnson, the American manager who moved from Tokyo to Beijing, explained in an interview the method he used when bringing Germans, Brazilians, Americans, and Indians together on one team. He recalled:

> When the team had its first face-to-face meeting, we invested half a day working in small break-out groups to create a team charter. We spent a full hour discussing what we wanted our conference calls and meetings to be like and what approach to timing we would follow. I asked them to decide as a group how they wanted to work together, and what level of flexibility versus structure they expected from one another during the meetings. We didn't talk at all about cultural differences in that meeting. We just talked about how we, this specific team, wanted to collaborate.

Having a clear discussion about scheduling systems up front can ease frustration that may otherwise pop up down the line. Having framed an agreement, the group can follow its own *team* culture instead of allowing members to follow the methods most natural in their home countries. After the team style has been created, the team leader will need to reinforce what the group has agreed and set aside time to revisit the agreement about twice a year, making any adaptations necessary.

## "YOUR WAY IS SO INEFFICIENT!"

Perhaps the most interesting thing about the Scheduling scale is that those from each side of the scale see those from the other side as inefficient and imagine they must lead lives that are terribly difficult and stressful.

When giving a talk about cultural differences during the trip to Indore, India, mentioned earlier, I had to constantly remind myself, "Flexibility is the key to success." Although I'd started my talk thirty-five minutes after the scheduled time, many participants arrived an hour late—or two—and others came and went at unforeseen moments, hearing my presentation in fits and starts. During this session, I told the story about my back-to-back presentations—the one in Denver orchestrated by Danielle with her time-tracking cards, and the one in Brazil that Ranato felt had been cut short inappropriately after just sixty-five minutes. I used the story, of course, to dramatize the extreme differences that cultures can exhibit when it comes to the Scheduling scale.

Afterward, a woman in her sixties, an accomplished psychologist garbed in a beautiful sari, came up to offer a comment. She'd been startled by my experience in Denver. "This type of rigidity that you have described to us about your American culture . . . it sounds extremely inefficient," she remarked. "All that time you spent rehearsing your presentation, getting the minutes down just right. It must be incredibly stressful and time-consuming to give a presentation in this type of environment. You must all get heart attacks! Yet the business culture of the U.S. has set an example for the rest of us for decades. I find it puzzling."

A response all but leapt to my lips. "No, no, no," I wanted to say (but restrained myself), "the system in my culture is an example of efficiency and relaxation. We set the plan, we prepare, we follow the plan. It is here, during this very session right now, when we are supposed to start at 9:00 a.m. but people arrive and leave (and come back again) at random. . . . *this* is what is inefficient and stressful. This is inefficient, because you are investing your time in coming to the session, but you are not getting what you are supposed to out of it, because you don't experience it from beginning to end . . . in order . . . one step at a (linear) time."

I opened my mouth to try to explain that, but I thought better of it. Instead, I invited this woman to go and stand with me in the evergreen-shaped line that was sprouting up at the coffee machine.

# Epilogue
## Putting the Culture Map to Work

When Ethan, my older son, was a baby, I invited a Danish colleague visiting Paris from Copenhagen over for dinner. It was a very cold January night, and Søren and I were talking in the kitchen while my husband dressed Ethan in the other room. After listening to my new-mother woes, Søren, who has three children, looked out onto our balcony and asked, "Do you give Ethan his naps outside or inside?"

I didn't understand the question. "Outside or inside of what?" I asked. It was so cold outside that I had put insulation around the door to keep the biting wind from whistling through the cracks. Was Søren suggesting I put our child out in the icy winter air for a two-hour nap? I wondered whether there was some fundamental rule of mothering that everyone had forgotten to tell me.

I was surprised when Søren explained that, in Denmark, it is quite common for parents to put their babies out in the winter afternoon for a nap. "We wrap them up and bring them in if it gets to be below minus ten degrees. It's good for them. They sleep better and they're less likely to get sick." Søren's minus ten was Celsius, the equivalent of fourteen degrees Fahrenheit. Even folks from my hometown in Minnesota would say "Brrr!"

A few years later, I got a call from a Danish woman who would be attending my weeklong course at INSEAD. "You asked us to prepare three things that are strange or surprising about our culture to share with the group on Monday evening," she said. "But I've thought a lot about it, and I can't think of anything unusual or strange about where I come from."

"Why don't you talk about putting your babies outside to nap on cold winter afternoons?" I suggested

"Would someone think that is strange?" she asked me, sounding utterly shocked. "Don't people do that in every country?"

The way we are conditioned to see the world in our own culture seems so completely obvious and commonplace that it is difficult to imagine that another culture might do things differently. It is only when you start to identify what is typical in your culture, but different from others, that you can begin to open a dialogue of sharing, learning, and ultimately understanding.

Of course, this book is not about babies, but about business. Yet the same rule applies: It is only when you start to identify what makes your culture different from others that you can begin to open a dialogue of sharing, learning, and ultimately understanding.

## PUTTING IT ALL TOGETHER: THE CULTURE MAP

Start by plotting your culture using the eight scales. You'll then have a map to compare your culture to those of your business partners. You can see how it works from the e-mail exchange I had with a French participant who had recently finished my course:

Hi, Erin,

After attending your presentation at our annual conference last week, I've been thinking about the invisible cultural boundaries impacting the effectiveness of my global team.

As you know, I'm a vice president at automotive supplier Valeo—a French company with big client bases in Germany and Japan, and a growing presence in China. I work frequently in all four countries and have people from each on my team.

When I moved to China, I thought the difficulty would be in bridging the cultural differences between Asians and Europeans. And it is true that the Asian members of my team are uncomfortable with the way our French and German members publicly disagree with them and give them negative feedback. I've coached the team members on how to moderate their approaches and reactions to work more effectively together.

But to my surprise, the most serious difficulties we have on the team are between the Chinese and the Japanese. The Chinese gripe that the Japanese are slow to make decisions, inflexible, and unwilling to change. The Japanese complain that the Chinese don't think things through, make rash decisions, and seem to thrive in chaos. Not only do these two Asian groups have difficulty working together, but the Japanese in many ways behave more like the Germans than like the Chinese—something I never anticipated.

I'd appreciate any thoughts and suggestions you may have.

Olivier

My response:

*Dear Olivier,*

*Start addressing your problem by creating a simple culture map using the scales outlined during my presentation. Plot out each culture on the eight scales and draw a broken line connecting all eight points. This line represents the overall pattern of that culture on the map. I've done that for you with the four cultures from your team.*

### FIGURE E.1.

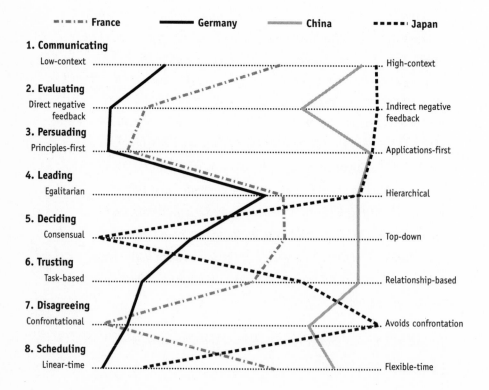

Now check the lines for Japan and China. On several scales,
they cluster together. As you've experienced, the Chinese and
Japanese are both uncomfortable with direct negative feedback
and open disagreement. That reflects the fact that, on scales two
(Evaluating) and seven (Disagreeing), the Europeans cluster
on one side and the Asian cultures on the other. Still, in most
cases, the Japanese perceive the Chinese as very direct—note the
difference between these cultures on scale two (Evaluating). The
French see the Germans in the same way.

Next, take a closer look at scales five (Deciding) and eight
(Scheduling), and you'll see the likely source of the frustration
on your team. Although Japan, like China, is very hierarchical
(scale four, Leading), it's a consensual society where decisions
are often made by the group in a bottom-up manner. That means
decisions take longer, as input from everyone is gathered and a
collective decision is formed. By contrast, in China, decisions are
most often made by the boss in a top-down fashion (scale five,
Deciding).

Furthermore, the Japanese have a linear-time culture (scale 8,
Scheduling). They build plans carefully and stick to the plan.
Being organized, structured, and on time are all values that
the Japanese share with their linear-time German colleagues.
Indeed, on both scales five (Deciding) and eight (Scheduling),
the Japanese are rather close to the German culture, farther from
France and quite far from China.

In comparison, the Chinese tend to make decisions quickly and to
change plans often and easily, valuing flexibility and adaptability

*over sticking to the plan. On these two scales (Deciding and Scheduling), the Chinese are closer to the French than to the Japanese.*

*Given these differences, it's understandable that your Japanese and Chinese team members are having difficulty working together. Can the problem be solved? Absolutely. The next step in improving these dynamics is to increase the awareness of your team members about how culture impacts their effectiveness.*

*Have your team read a couple of chapters from this book, or describe a few of the concepts yourself. Then discuss cultural differences at one of your team meetings or over a team dinner. Ask questions like:*

- *Do you agree with the positions as outlined in this chapter? Why or why not?*
- *What else can you share with the group so that we better understand your own culture's positioning on this scale?*
- *Do you think these concepts are impacting our team's collaboration?*
- *What can we do to be more effective, given these differences?*

*It doesn't matter whether your team members agree with what they've read; what's important is to start exploring and discussing the differences in value systems and work methods. Just as fish don't know they're in water, people often find it difficult to see and recognize their own culture until they start comparing it with others.*

*Be sure to conduct the discussion with humility and without
judgment. The more you can joke about your own culture and
speak positively about the ways other cultures operate, the easier
it will be for everyone to share their thoughts and opinions
without becoming defensive.*

*The more aware the team becomes of how culture is impacting
their work, the more effective they will be at bridging the
differences. The French expression* Quand on connait
sa maladie, on est a moitié guérie *(Once you identify
your sickness, you are halfway cured) certainly applies to
multicultural teamwork. Help your team articulate the cultural
differences that are impacting their effectiveness, and they will
begin to work better together.*

*I hope some of these ideas will help improve your team
effectiveness. Please keep in touch and let me know how it goes.*

*Erin*

## BRIDGING THE FAULT LINES

If you face cultural challenges similar to those that troubled
Olivier, try applying the same strategy. Create a culture map that
enables an easy visual comparison of the various cultures represented in your team. Noting the points of similarity and difference
will help you recognize the fault lines that may be dividing your
team members—invisible psychological boundaries that separate
groups, creating an "us versus them" mentality.

As you build your own awareness, you will be better able to
act as a cultural bridge. Help your team members develop their

cultural flexibility by coaching them to suspend their judgments and see the situation from an opposing perspective.

When invisible cultural barriers impact a global team, you'll often find that each group is frustrated with the other's approach. The more they complain, the bigger the fault line becomes. One way you can deal with this is by organizing the team so that there is less cultural homogeneity at each location. This can help to break down the us-versus-them divide. Olivier, for example, might want to have Germans, French, and Chinese all living and working together in Japan. It can also be helpful to rotate your team members when possible so a number of them spend a few months, or even years, at other locations.

Another valuable step is hiring people who are bicultural or have extensive experience living in more than one culture represented on your team. If you make a good choice and train that person well, he can play a critical role in helping one group decode the other's behavior.

Sometimes cultural diversity on global teams creates fault lines, but other times that same level of diversity can be a great advantage. For example, suppose you are handed a project that has dozens of drop-dead deadlines and that therefore requires a linear-time approach. Get those people on your team with strong linear-time preferences to own that project. Another time you may have a client who is constantly changing his mind and serving him well requires flexibility and comfort with changing routes at the drop of a hat. Having team members who are strongly flexible-time (both because of their culture as well as their personalities) will help meet your client's needs.

Sometimes, you may feel as if you really need direct negative feedback about how to improve something that you can't get right.

Having people with a frank feedback style who are from direct cultures on the Evaluating scale will be invaluable. At other times, you might need a small group of people to give negative feedback to a sensitive and valued client and to do it with the utmost delicacy. Here is an opportunity to call on the strength of those individuals who are pros at indirect negative feedback.

So when you look at your team's culture map, consider not just the difficulties that might arise from the gaps but also the strengths that the differences may provide. Managed with care, the cultural and individual diversity can become your team's greatest asset.

## WE ARE ALL THE SAME, WE ARE ALL DIFFERENT

During a course on multicultural negotiations, a young MBA student from Ukraine approached me during a break and asked me urgently, "Erin, you have been talking about the importance of cultural differences, yet I have always believed that no matter where we come from, humans are fundamentally all the same. Isn't this true?"

Later that morning, I was buttonholed by a group of students from India who had been talking excitedly. "We are in the middle of a debate," one of them declared. "As we have seen this morning, culture seems to have a big impact on business behavior. Yet last week, our whole class took a personality assessment, and we saw that the six of us—who are all from the same part of India—each have very different personalities. Isn't every individual different?"

The answer to both of these questions is, of course, yes.

It's true that human beings are fundamentally the same. At a deep level, no matter where we come from, people are driven by common physiological and psychological needs and motivations.

When we are nervous or elated, we all find our hearts beating faster. When we are gloomy or depressed, we all feel enervated and exhausted. We all feel common human emotions such as jealousy, excitement, sorrow, and passion. At a deep level, we are all the same species. In this sense, no matter which culture we come from, humans are the same.

And, yes, every individual is different. Even when raised in the same community, by the same parents, working in the same environment, no two individuals are precisely the same; each of us has a unique style and set of preferences, interests, aversions, and values.

So no matter who you are working with or where that person comes from, you should begin any relationship with the desire to understand what is specific and unique to that individual. Don't assume that you can determine anything specific about how they will think or behave from what you know about their cultural background.

Yet the culture in which we grow up has a profound impact on how we see the world. In any given culture, members are conditioned to understand the world in a particular way, to see certain communication patterns as effective or undesirable, to find certain arguments persuasive or lacking merit, to consider certain ways of making decisions or measuring time "natural" or "strange."

Leaders have always needed to understand human nature and personality differences to be successful in business—that's nothing new. What's new is the requirement for twenty-first century leaders to be prepared to understand a wider, richer array of work styles than ever before and to be able to determine what aspects of an interaction are simply a result of personality and which are a result of differences in cultural perspective.

When we worked in offices surrounded by others from our own tribe, awareness of basic human psychological needs and motivations, as well as a sensitivity to individual differences was enough. But as globalization transforms the way we work, we now need the ability to decode cultural differences in order to work effectively with clients, suppliers, and colleagues from around the world.

Challenging? Yes! But it's also fascinating. The range of human cultures can be a source of endless surprise and discovery—a fount of remarkable experiences and continual learning that can never be exhausted.

# ACKNOWLEDGMENTS

Like most authors, I owe an enormous debt of gratitude to a number of people whose help and support have made this book possible.

Thanks first of all to my excellent editor at PublicAffairs, John Mahaney. John managed to see promise in a first book chapter, which was very rough. He provided careful and insightful guidance throughout the writing process. He encouraged me to write from my own viewpoint, and he showed me, paragraph by paragraph, how to put color into my storytelling and make my examples more engaging. It wouldn't be the same book without John.

A big ribbon-wrapped thanks to my literary agent, Carol Franco, who has also had an enormous impact on this book. Not only did Carol find the best publisher I could hope for, she stood beside me through two years of trials and uncertainty. When I needed advice from an expert, Carol was always ready and waiting with supportive and lucid guidance.

Thanks to Karl Weber, a terrific editor, who took a manuscript that was often too long and frequently too wordy and gave it a serious polish. If it weren't for Karl, this book would be a whole lot more dull. It is thanks to him that the reader was saved multiple painful anecdotes such as the one about the fly who buzzed around the world viewing classrooms in different countries and the man who visited a doctor in rural China to get help with his foot only to have the doctor look at his tongue.

Thanks also to Elin Williams, the writer and editor whose assistance first made me realize that with really good help, I could write a book. Elin invested much time in learning about my work before we even started and then helped me through the entire first draft, skillfully editing every chapter.

Thanks to Stuart Crainer and Des Dearlove, who helped me get this project off the ground in the first place. They worked with me to outline the book's content and sketch out the various chapters. Stuart and Des came up with the book title and wrote the first draft of the book proposal. They read versions of the first few chapters many times and provided support in the early days.

Thanks to my mother, Linda Burkett, not only because she has been a fundamental point of love and support for forty-two years, but because she has read versions of each chapter far more times than anyone else. She has been my professional confidante all along the way, weighing each example I was uncertain about, fixing any passage I couldn't get quite right, and taking phone calls at 6:00 a.m. to weigh in on a new title idea or yet another cover design. Next to myself, my mother is the person who has devoted the most time to this book.

Now to the rest of my family, who put up with me throughout an arduous and sometimes trying process. I owe you a heartfelt thank you, which doesn't have anything specific to do with the book but everything to do with the daily support you provide for all I do. I couldn't have written this book without the support of my gaggle of boys—my husband, Eric, and our two sons, Ethan and Logan. The three of you are the foundation of everything good in my life. A big thanks to my father, Tim, who has taught me to be tenacious, and through his unwavering belief in me has taught me to believe in myself. Thanks also to my brother Jed and his wife, Seema, for demonstrating how to meet life's unexpected challenges with grace and persistence. And a thank you to my close friend Jennifer, whose multicultural journey has often paralleled my own.

When I finished the first draft of this book, I was excited to get feedback. I sent the manuscript out to a number of colleagues who have specific expertise in various world regions. Each of them painstakingly read the manuscript and provided corrections and suggestions. Thanks to Mary Yoko Brannen, Elisabeth Shen, Edith Coron, Philippe Aboubadra, Monika Stok, Sabine Havenstein, Stanislav Shekshnia, Martina Harms, and Gisela Henrique for all the time you devoted to this project.

The team at PublicAffairs has consistently exceeded all of my expectations. Thank you to Jaime Leifer, Melissa Veronesi, Melissa Raymond, Victoria Gilder, and the many other individuals who have given their care and attention to this book.

Thanks also to the people who inspired me. Thanks to Geert Hofstede, Fons Trompenaars, and Edward Hall, who were writing about this subject long before me and whose work provided the foundation for many of the concepts in this book. Thank you to Henry Zinglersen, who introduced me to many of the concepts that appear in this book. It was Henry's early mentoring that led me to the eight scales. Thanks to my colleague and mentor at INSEAD, Herminia Ibarra, who encouraged me to write this book and had enough faith in my work to introduce me to both Elin Williams and Carol Franco.

Most of all, thanks to the thousands of executive students who have participated in my sessions and shared their experiences and perspectives, both inside and outside of INSEAD, thus providing the basis for every example and strategy present in this book.

# NOTES

## INTRODUCTION

1. I first heard this analogy from my colleague and mentor, Professor Jose Santos, who speaks about the similarity between culture and water in his courses. The analogy is also referenced in the book by Fons Trompenaars and Charles Hampden-Turner, *Riding the Waves of Culture: Understanding Diversity in Global Business*, 2nd ed. (New York: McGraw Hill, 1998), who wrote: "A fish only discovers its need for water when it is no longer in it. Our own culture is like water to a fish. We live and breathe through it." Just recently, after the first draft of this book was complete, author Kai Hammerich and Richard Lewis titled their new book after this analogy, *Fish Can't See Water: How National Culture Can Make or Break Your Corporate Strategy* (Wiley, 2013).

## CHAPTER 1

1. Edward T. Hall, *Beyond Culture* (1976; New York: Anchor Books, 1989), 85–125.

2. This same dialogue in various formats has been told to me several times. The first time was by Denise Austin Guillon, an American consultant living in Paris, who included a similar dialogue in a presentation I attended many years ago.

## CHAPTER 2

1. This translation guide has been circulated in various forms anonymously on the Internet. One idea is that it was originally developed by Shell Oil Co. to help their employees better understand one another.

2. Adapted from Vladimir Zhelvis, *Xenophobe's Guide to the Russians* (2001; London: Oval Books, 2010).

## CHAPTER 3

1. Richard Nisbett, *The Geography of Thought* (New York: The Free Press, 2003), 48–78.

2. Richard Nisbett and Takahiko Masuda, "Culture and Point of View" (Special series of Inaugural Articles by members of the National Academy of Sciences), *PNAS* 100, no. 19 (September 2003): 11163–11170.

## CHAPTER 4

1. Geert Hofstede, Gert Jan Hofstede, and Michael Minkov, *Cultures and Organizations: Software of the Mind* (1991; New York: McGraw Hill, 2010), 53–88.

2. Robert House, Paul Hanges, Mansour Javidan, Peter Dorfman, and Vipin Gupta, *Culture, Leadership, and Organizations: The GLOBE Study of 62 Societies* (Thousand Oaks, CA: Sage), 513–563.

3. André Laurent, "The Cross-Cultural Puzzle of International Human Resource Management," *Human Resource Management* 25, no. 1 (Spring 1986): 91–102.

## CHAPTER 5

1. Patrick Lencioni is the author of ten business books including best sellers *The Five Dysfunctions of a Team* (San Francisco, CA: Jossey-Bass, 2002), and *The Advantage: Why Organizational Health Trumps Everything Else in Business* (San Francisco, CA: Jossey-Bass), 2012.

2. For more about the Japanese decision-making process, see Sue Shinomiya and Brian Szepkowski, *Passport to Japan: Revised and Updated Edition* (Berkeley, CA: Stonebridge Press, 2007), 100–103.

3. Many of these recommendations first appeared in Dr. Ernest Gundling, *Communicating with the Japanese in Business*, distributed by JETRO, 1999, 10–11.

## CHAPTER 6

1. Roy Y. J. Chua, "Building Effective Business Relationships in China," *MIT Sloan Management Review* 53, no. 4 (Summer 2012), and Crystal Jiang, Roy Y. J. Chua, Masaaki Kotabe, and Janet Murray, "Effects of Cultural Ethnicity, Firm Size, and Firm Age on Senior Executives' Trust in Their Overseas Business Partners: Evidence from China," *Journal of International Business Studies* 42, no. 9 (2011): 1150–1173. Roy Y. J.

Chua, Michael W. Morris and Paul Ingram, "*Guanxi* vs. Networking: Distinctive Configurations of Affect-and Cognition-based Trust in the Networks of Chinese vs. American Managers," *Journal of International Business Studies* (2009) 40, 490–508. doi: 10.1057/palgrave.jibs.8400422.

2. Kurt Lewin, "Some Social-Psychological Differences between the United States and Germany," *Character and Personality* 4 (1936).

3. Fons Trompenaars and Charles Hampden-Turner, *Riding the Waves of Culture: Understanding Diversity in Global Business*, 2nd ed. (New York: McGraw Hill, 1998), 83–86.

4. Roderick Swaab, William Maddux, and Marwan Sinaceur, "Virtual Linguistic Mimicry: When and How Online Mimicry Increases Negotiation Outcomes," *Journal of Experimental Social Psychology* 47 (2011): 616–621.

### CHAPTER 7

1.  Suleman Shahid, Emiel Krahmer, and Marc Swerts, *Fun and Games: Springer Proceedings of the Second Edition of the International Conference* (Eindhoven, the Netherlands: 2008, Series: Springer—LNCS). Book chapter "Alone or Together: Exploring the Effect of Physical Co-presence on the Emotional Expressions of Game Playing Children Across Cultures," 94–105.

### CHAPTER 8

1. Edward T. Hall, *The Dance of Life: The Other Dimension of Time* (1983; New York: Anchor Books, 1989), 44–58.

2. Robert Levine, *The Geography of Time: The Temporal Misadventures of a Social Psychologist* (New York: Basic Books, 1997), 81–100.

3. This evergreen line was written about in the *New York Times* by Anand Giridharads, "Getting In and Out of Line," *New York Times*, August 7, 2010.

# INDEX

An American based in France, **Erin Meyer** is a professor at INSEAD, one of the world's leading international business schools. She is program director for INSEAD's Managing Global Virtual Teams and Management Skills for International Business executive education programs. She has written for the *Harvard Business Review, Singapore Business Times,* and Forbes.com. In 2013 Erin was selected for the Thinkers50 Radar list of the world's up-and-coming business thinkers.

PublicAffairs is a publishing house founded in 1997. It is a tribute to the standards, values, and flair of three persons who have served as mentors to countless reporters, writers, editors, and book people of all kinds, including me.

I. F. STONE, proprietor of *I. F. Stone's Weekly*, combined a commitment to the First Amendment with entrepreneurial zeal and reporting skill and became one of the great independent journalists in American history. At the age of eighty, Izzy published *The Trial of Socrates*, which was a national bestseller. He wrote the book after he taught himself ancient Greek.

BENJAMIN C. BRADLEE was for nearly thirty years the charismatic editorial leader of *The Washington Post*. It was Ben who gave the *Post* the range and courage to pursue such historic issues as Watergate. He supported his reporters with a tenacity that made them fearless and it is no accident that so many became authors of influential, best-selling books.

ROBERT L. BERNSTEIN, the chief executive of Random House for more than a quarter century, guided one of the nation's premier publishing houses. Bob was personally responsible for many books of political dissent and argument that challenged tyranny around the globe. He is also the founder and longtime chair of Human Rights Watch, one of the most respected human rights organizations in the world.

·    ·    ·

For fifty years, the banner of Public Affairs Press was carried by its owner Morris B. Schnapper, who published Gandhi, Nasser, Toynbee, Truman, and about 1,500 other authors. In 1983, Schnapper was described by *The Washington Post* as "a redoubtable gadfly." His legacy will endure in the books to come.

Peter Osnos, *Founder and Editor-at-Large*